HEROES OF HISTORY

ELIZABETH FRY

Angel of Newgate

JANET & GEOFF BENGE

Emerald Books

P.O. BOX 635, LYNNWOOD, WA 98046

Emerald Books are distributed through YWAM Publishing. For a full list of titles, including other great biographies, visit our website at www.emeraldbooks.com.

Elizabeth Fry: Angel of Newgate

Published by Emerald Books
P.O. Box 635
Lynnwood, WA 98046

Library of Congress Cataloging-in-Publication Data
Benge, Janet, 1958–
Elizabeth Fry : angel of newgate / Janet and Geoff Benge.
pages cm.—(Heroes of history)
Includes bibliographical references.
ISBN 978-1-62486-064-5 (pbk.)—ISBN 978-1-62486-065-2 (e-book)
1. Fry, Elizabeth Gurney, 1780–1845. 2. Prison reformers—Great Britain—Biography—Juvenile literature. I. Benge, Geoff, 1954– II. Title.
HV8978.F7B46 2015
365'.92—dc23
[B] 2015004182

Second printing 2021

ISBN 978-1-62486-064-5 (paperback)
ISBN 978-1-62486-065-2 (e-book)

Printed in the United States of America

HEROES OF HISTORY

ELIZABETH FRY

Angel of Newgate

HEROES OF HISTORY

Abraham Lincoln
Alan Shepard
Ben Carson
Benjamin Franklin
Benjamin Rush
Billy Graham
Captain John Smith
Christopher Columbus
Clara Barton
Davy Crockett
Daniel Boone
Douglas MacArthur
Dwight Eisenhower
Elizabeth Fry
Ernest Shackleton
George Washington
George Washington Carver
Harriet Tubman
John Adams
Laura Ingalls Wilder
Louis Zamperini
Meriwether Lewis
Milton Hershey
Orville Wright
Ronald Reagan
Theodore Roosevelt
Thomas Edison
William Bradford
William Penn
William Wilberforce

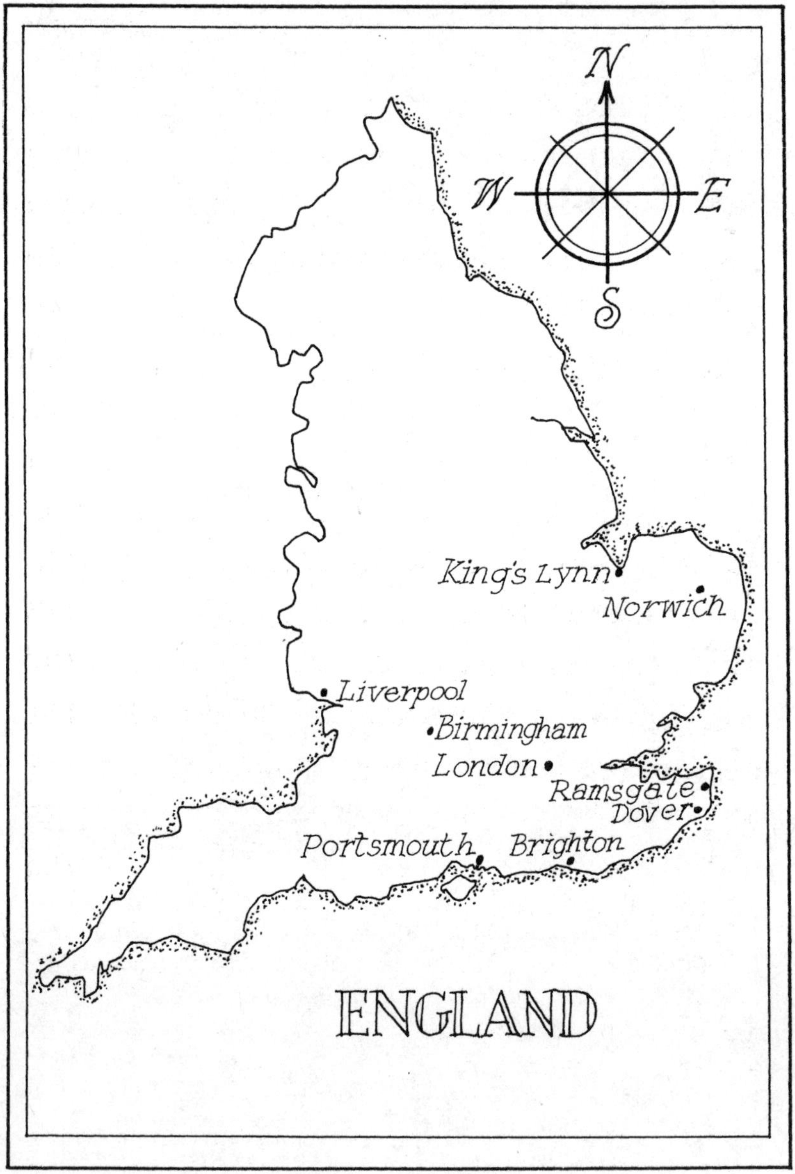
N
W
E
S
King's Lynn
Norwich
Liverpool
Birmingham
London
Ramsgate
Dover
Portsmouth
Brighton
ENGLAND

Contents

Chapter 1

Earlham Hall

Six-year-old Elizabeth Gurney, or Betsy, as everyone called her, ran from room to room. She wanted to catch one last glimpse of her old home before the coach came to take her away. She bumped into her grandmother in the hallway. "Slow down, child. You'll fall and hurt yourself."

Betsy smiled. Her grandmother, whom she was named after, was a stout old woman dressed in a plain gray dress and starched white bonnet. Betsy knew she would miss her a lot. Indeed, she would miss many things about living at Gurney Court on Magdalen Street in Norwich.

Betsy had always shared an upstairs bedroom with her two older sisters, Catherine (or Kitty, as she was known) and Rachel. The bedroom window commanded a wonderful view of the narrow, cobbled street below. Now, as she peeked through the curtains one last time, Betsy watched as a horse and cart plodded past. The cart was loaded with sacks of coal. Since it was Tuesday, Betsy knew that the coal was being delivered to the large haberdashery on the corner. A dog darted between the buggy traffic on the street, and an old woman with a walking stick hobbled toward the house. One-armed Betty, everyone called her. She often stopped outside the Gurney home, where Betsy's mother, Catherine Gurney, would give her food wrapped in a kerchief. Betsy suspected there was often a penny tied in the corner of the kerchief as well. Her mother was like that—always making sure the poor people in town had enough to eat. "'Tis thy duty to help the poor. We cannot help the whole of England, but we can help our neighbors," she would say to Betsy as she made up a basket of food for some needy family.

Sometimes Betsy would accompany her mother on short walks along Norwich's busy streets to deliver food, something she loved to do. But now it was all over. Betsy's entire life was about to change as she—along with her two big sisters; her younger brother, John; her four little sisters, Richenda, Hannah, Louisa, and Priscilla; and their parents—was moving out to a large country estate called Earlham located on the west side of town. Betsy tried to understand why they had to move. She gathered it had something to do with the ever-growing size of the Gurney family. In fact, she had seen her mother mending the skirting around the cradle just last week, and her mother had confided to her that another baby was on the way. Betsy wondered whether it would be a boy or a girl. The only brother she had was John, who was a year younger than she. An earlier son, who was also named John, had died before Betsy was born. All she knew of him was his tiny grave at the Quaker burial ground on Chather Street.

"Seven little girls!" Betsy often heard people exclaim, especially at the Quaker meetinghouse they attended. "And all with red or golden hair. Whoever heard of such a thing?" Betsy's mother would laugh at such comments and respond, "They are a handful to keep clothed and neat, but I wouldn't be without one of them."

Betsy knew that her mother was telling the truth. Their home was a happy one. Betsy's father, John Gurney, belonged to a wealthy family who owned woolen mills in the area. He came from a long line of Quakers, as did Betsy's mother. Catherine Gurney's family had been prominent Quakers, and Catherine could trace her family line back to her great-grandfather, Robert Barclay, a famous and heroic early Quaker. Barclay had traveled with William Penn, who had gone on to found the colony of Pennsylvania in North America.

Now, in 1786, Betsy's parents insisted that all the children accompany them every Sunday morning to the meeting in the Quaker meetinghouse at Goat Lane, and Catherine Gurney read a passage from the Bible to the children each morning after breakfast. Although the Gurneys practiced a more modern form of Quakerism and did not keep many of the rules of the Plain Quakers, Betsy knew all about the older Plain Quaker ways. Plain Quakers were people such as her grandmother and her uncle Joseph, her father's brother. Uncle Joseph, who lived with them in the house at Norwich, wore a plain black vest and topcoat over a collarless white shirt and a black, wide-brimmed hat. He wouldn't remove his hat even when he was indoors, and he refused to take off his hat when he met someone who was more important than he was. He spoke using "thees" and "thous" because these forms were once the way English speakers addressed an equal, while addressing an individual as "you" signaled a respect Plain Quakers thought was improper.

Everyone, including Betsy's father, thought all this to be bad manners. Uncle Joseph and the Plain Quakers disagreed. For generations, Quakers had refused to practice "hat honor" or use special polite speech for people of higher social rank as a protest against the idea that some people are superior. They believed all people carried the inward light of Jesus Christ, and no one should respect a person or class of people over another. All people should be addressed and treated in the same manner.

"Betsy, come downstairs. It's time to go," Betsy heard her mother call. Soon the entire family was seated in the coach, being pulled to their new home by six handsome black horses.

Betsy tried not to think about the previous time she had attempted to get into the coach. She was not proud of her behavior then, and it was hard for her to explain the fear that had washed over her that day. The Gurney family had been preparing for an outing to visit distant relatives in the country, and Betsy was the last to get into the coach. As she climbed into the carriage, she was overcome with fear. She ran back inside the house and sat weeping in the corner of the kitchen. Every time her mother or father approached, she shrieked with fear. Eventually the whole outing was called off, and it took Betsy many hours to feel calm again.

Betsy had heard Kitty ask their mother what was wrong with Betsy. "It's just her affliction," her mother replied. "She's afraid of so many things." Betsy felt ashamed at the response, but she knew her mother was right. The long drapes in her room at night turned into tall soldiers with swords, the twisting hallways in the house echoed with the footsteps of ghosts, and every time she heard a dog howl in the night she wondered if the door had been properly barred. She was quite sure her sisters and brother didn't worry about these things as she did. Fear and worry were her "affliction," something she found ways to deal with most of the time, like today as the family rode along toward their new home.

"Look, I can see it!" Hannah said, tugging at Betsy's sleeve. "Our new house. It's so big. It has four sets of chimneys."

Betsy smiled. Hannah was right. The coach rolled down a driveway lined with elm trees, winding through beautiful parkland and coming to a stop in front of an enormous redbrick building that dated back two hundred years—Earlham Hall.

Betsy's mother and Hannah Judd, their faithful housekeeper, took several days to transfer all of the Gurney family's furniture and other belongings into the new home. During this time Betsy's mother allowed the children to explore their new surroundings. The house itself was big and sprawling, with attics, winding passageways, staircases, and large cupboards and closets. Outside, it was surrounded by gardens and green lawns fringed by trees. Beyond the trees was open pasture speckled with colorful wildflowers. Stables and a coach house, along with a workshop and the laundry, stood nearby. A short distance from Earlham Hall was the Yare River, where the children could play and sail boats. And while she hadn't been eager to leave her grandmother's house in Norwich, Betsy had to admit that the surroundings of their new house were wonderful.

Once the house was put in order, it was time for school. When the family lived at Gurney Court, Catherine Gurney had taught her two oldest daughters Latin, French, English, history, geography, and mathematics. Now it was time for Betsy to take her place at the study table. While Betsy had looked forward to this, her dreams of being a good student were soon dashed. Unlike Kitty and Rachel, she was not, as her mother put it, "a natural learner." Learning to read took a long time, and Betsy gave up on the idea of ever being a good speller. Languages were almost impossible to remember, and her brain often confused the order of numbers in mathematics, making her feel foolish.

The only subject Betsy enjoyed was history. This was partly because of the exciting times in which she lived. Her mother wrote down the word *revolution*.

"That," she said, "means turning something upside down—that something has been the same way for a very long time, and then all of a sudden everything is on its head and quite different." Betsy thought this definition through. Her mother had read her stories about the American Revolution and how the colonists in North America had risen up and fought and defeated the British military forces five years earlier, winning their independence from Great Britain. Revolution, indeed.

Betsy was grateful that Catherine Gurney did not make her children study for too long each day, leaving them plenty of time to play. Earlham Hall offered endless opportunities for games, such as hide-and-seek. Betsy and her sisters once decided to count every cupboard in the house—but they gave up after eighty. The house had been added on to and altered so many times that there were nooks and crannies everywhere. Betsy liked to join in the games, but sometimes she became scared when she was not "found" for a long time. Often at night she imagined people staring in the windows at her or ghosts in the corner of the living room, lurking in the shadows beyond the light of the candles. Betsy was always embarrassed that none of her family members, not even the youngest children, were concerned about such things.

In the fall, Betsy's mother gave birth to another child, a boy named Samuel. Two years later, when Betsy was eight years old, another son, Joseph John, was born. By the time little Joseph arrived, Betsy was doing better with her reading and writing, and she was able to start keeping a diary every day like her older sisters did. Her diary entries contained lots of spelling errors, but most of the time Betsy could work out what she wanted to say. She wrote about riding the pet ponies her father had bought for the children to ride in the meadow, collecting bluebells and daffodils, and roasting potatoes in the glowing embers of fires at the end of the garden. She also wrote about the interesting stream of visitors who came to Earlham Hall for an afternoon or a week. Many were Quakers her parents were expected to show hospitality to, but others were from different walks of life—Catholics and Protestants whose company her parents enjoyed.

Betsy also wrote about the endless hours she and her nine siblings spent at the Quaker meetinghouse on Goat Lane in Norwich. Once or twice a week, the family rode into Norwich to take their seats at the meeting—men on the left, women on the right. As much as Betsy wanted to please her mother, she found sitting still for long periods of time next to impossible. Since the Quakers had no paid clergy, anyone was free to stand and speak during a service "if the Spirit moved them." As far as Betsy could see, this meant long silences when everyone was supposed to be praying. Sometimes an hour would pass before anyone spoke, while other times no one said a word, and the meeting was dismissed.

During the meetings Betsy perfected the art of praying with her eyes slightly open so she could look around and see what everyone else was doing. Her mother always looked serene. Her father, on the other hand, often opened his eyes and looked bored—but not as bored as the Gurney children. It was hard not to giggle and pinch each other once in a while. The children developed code words to use in their diaries to describe their days. Betsy often wrote, "Goats was dis," which meant that a Quaker meeting was particularly unpleasant.

In May 1791, when Betsy was nearly eleven years old, her mother again gave birth to a baby boy, who was named Daniel. Betsy had spent much of the time during her mother's pregnancy fretting that something would happen to her mom or the unborn baby. She sometimes tiptoed into the bedroom to see whether her mother was still breathing, and she prayed that her mother would not trip when she walked up or down the stairs. Although Daniel was born without incident, Betsy still could not shake the feeling that something terrible was about to happen.

Chapter 2

A Ship without a Pilot

Betsy sat by the fire writing in her diary. "October 26, 1792. Mother is unwell and did not leave her bed. Kitty conducted classes, and the little ones were allowed to bundle up and accompany father to Norwich in the sleigh. Daniel, of course, was with nurse Sarah."

Betsy then picked up a piece of needlepoint she had just begun. Rachel read aloud from Livy's *Roman History*. Normally this was one of the happiest times of the day for Betsy, who loved to listen to others read, but tonight was different. It was not unusual for her mother to be in bed. Her twelve pregnancies had come with their share of illnesses. Kitty had asked their father if another baby might be on the way. John shook his head and said, "It's some kind of fever your mother has. If she isn't better tomorrow,

I will fetch Dr. Alderson." This relieved Betsy a little. James Alderson and his daughter Amelia were regular visitors at the Earlham estate, and Betsy trusted the doctor.

The following day brought no improvement in Catherine Gurney's condition. Dr. Alderson was called, and again the day after that. All sorts of poultices were made and applied to Betsy's mother in the hope of curing her illness, but nothing seemed to help.

Two weeks later, Catherine was weak and delirious. It was difficult for Betsy to sit in the room with her, watching her mother fight to get out of bed and kneel beside it in prayer. The words that tumbled from Catherine's lips were always the same: Catherine prayed for Kitty, John, and Joseph John. Betsy knew that her mother had little control over what she was saying, but it crushed her to think that of her eleven children her mother could remember only three of them in her delirious state. At night Betsy tried to make sense of it: Did her mother see hope for only those three of her children? Were they the ones who would make something of their lives? Or worse, were most of the children going to die soon, leaving only Kitty, John, and Joseph John to carry on to adulthood?

Such grim thoughts, along with the fear that despite the best medicines available, her mother might not recover, disturbed twelve-year-old Betsy. Betsy watched anxiously for clues as to what her father was thinking. What she saw disturbed her even more. At the beginning of November her father had stopped all his business dealings in Norwich, instead staying home, where he would alternately sit beside his wife's bed and pace under her window with his hunting dogs.

It felt to Betsy like the entire house was holding its breath. Everyone tiptoed through the hallways, and Mrs. Judd, their Quaker housekeeper, prayed constantly. But it did no good. On November 17, 1792, Catherine Bell Gurney whispered her final words, "Peace, sweet is peace," and slipped away, dying at age thirty-nine.

When all the children gathered around the bed to say goodbye to their deceased mother, Betsy stood back. She could not believe she was looking at the person she loved most in the world. It was as if a light had gone out in her soul. Betsy struggled through the rest of the day, greeting groups of relatives and Quaker friends who arrived to pay their respects. Two days later, on a cold, damp morning, her mother was laid to rest in the Quaker burial ground on Chather Street. A cold shadow passed over Betsy as she thought about the individuals around her ending up buried beneath the same plot of earth.

Betsy knew that these thoughts were morbid, but she could not contain them. Nighttime became a test of endurance, where the same dream repeatedly haunted her. She was standing on a deserted beach on a windy night. As she watched the waves crash onto the stony shore, she lost her footing and slowly began to sink into the sea. The frigid water foamed around her as she struggled to get back onto firm ground. As she grasped for the shore, her hands filled with stones. Deeper and deeper she slid until her head went under. Everything was silent and dark. She could not breathe. She let go of the stones and surrendered to death. That was the exact moment when Betsy would awake in a sweat, her heart thumping. The dream was so vivid that she could almost feel the salt water in her nostrils and the seaweed tangled in her long, golden hair. Then, silently, so as not to wake her sisters, Betsy would weep for her mother, for her widowed father, for her baby brother Daniel, who would have no memory of his mother, and for herself. By the time daylight shone through the opening between the drapes, Betsy had again gained control of herself.

As the weeks passed, the dream continued, though during the day Betsy was able to participate in family activities. This was because with their mother gone there was much to do. Betsy's father asked that Kitty, Betsy's older sister, take over the role of mothering the ten other children. Kitty agreed and was given the title "Mrs. Catherine Gurney." It signified the end of her childhood and, since she would be responsible for Daniel for the next fifteen years, also put an end to any thought of her marrying.

In her new role, Kitty relied heavily on Rachel and Betsy to help run the house. She often called them into her sitting room for conferences about the younger children's schooling or outings. She had a lot to plan. John was now away at boarding school in London, but nine children (not including Kitty) were still in the home.

Life at Earlham Hall soon developed a new pattern not too different from the old one. The school-aged children started their lessons early in the morning while Sarah Williman, the nurse, watched Daniel and Joseph John. Then there was needlepoint, lunch, music, art lessons, and a walk before dinner.

John Gurney left most of the decisions about the children in Kitty's hands. The girls chose to wear bright-colored clothes—their most fashionable outfits—to the Quaker meetings on Sunday mornings. Betsy knew that many of their Plain Quaker relatives, including Uncle Joseph, did not approve of the way they lived. Betsy's favorite outfit, which Uncle Joseph never failed to frown upon, included bright red boots with purple laces. On summer days the older girls rode horses into Norwich to stroll down the streets and buy whatever they fancied.

By 1795, when Betsy was fifteen years old, she had even more reason to visit Norwich: British soldiers. In 1789 a revolution in France had swept aside the French monarchy and established a new republic. French troops began to expand across Europe, conquering country after country, spreading revolutionary fervor across the continent. For the previous two years, Great Britain had been fighting France to stop their advance in Europe. However, many people in and around Norwich declared themselves to be Republicans—British citizens who sympathized with the aims of the French Revolution, especially doing away with the monarchy. As a result, King George III worried that if the French decided to try to invade England, they would find many people in and around Norwich who would shelter and encourage them. To guard against this possibility, British troops were quartered throughout East Anglia, the region where Norwich was located.

The Gurney girls loved to watch the soldiers parade through Norwich wearing their bright red uniforms with tall felt hats and carrying shiny muskets. Of course, this was something else Uncle Joseph disapproved of. Because most Quakers were pacifists, they did not believe in going to war, since it might lead them to kill someone. Besides, didn't the Bible tell them to turn the other cheek? But by now none of the Gurney children, including Betsy, cared too much about the Quaker view of anything. It was not long before the military officers were invited to music and dance evenings at Earlham Hall.

It seemed to Betsy that her father would spare no expense to see his girls happy. John always served the best food and drinks to the young people who came to visit. Most of the time Betsy thoroughly enjoyed herself, except when she was in one of her dark moods, as she called them. A dark mood could last a day, a week, or even a month, and it colored the way Betsy looked at everything. Betsy became gloomy and found it hard to understand why she was even alive. Everything in her life—the dancing, her schooling, and especially Quaker meetings—seemed pointless. During such times her nightmares would return, and she often had to spend entire days in bed. The rest of the Gurney family seemed to work around her. It appeared to Betsy that no one understood her except her little brother Joseph John, who also suffered from nightmares.

Time passed, and Betsy and her father went to London to meet with a highly recommended doctor to see what he could do for Betsy's moods. The doctor offered no help. Betsy found that writing in her diary about how she felt offered the most relief. Sometimes her entries were about dashing soldiers and lively dances. Other times she wondered if those pursuits were taking her in the wrong direction. On May 21, 1797, her seventeenth birthday, she wrote, "I hope I shall be much better this day [a year from] now, I hope to be quite an altered person; to have more knowledge, to have my mind in greater order, and my heart too, that wants to be put in order as much [as], if not more, than any part of me, it is in such a fly-away state."

Part of that fly-away state revolved around a certain military officer named James Lloyd, himself a Quaker and the son of a large Birmingham banking family. James took an immediate interest in Betsy, who soon was sure she was in love. Soon after this, however, Betsy fell into a deep depression and was unable to leave the house. Every bone in her body ached, and she was sure she was about to die. Not surprisingly, Betsy found James backing away from his plan to woo her.

At this time Betsy's sister Rachel also fell in love, with a local young man named Henry Enfield, the son of a local minister. Henry and his sister had been regular visitors at Earlham Hall for many years. There was one problem with Rachel and Henry falling in love—he was not a Quaker, and marrying outside the Quaker faith was forbidden. If Rachel married Henry, she would be disowned by the church, and all family ties would be severed. Not only that, but her action would cause a shadow to fall over the whole Gurney family, affecting business and social arrangements. As a result, Rachel begged her sisters to keep her love for Henry a secret. Betsy kept her sister's secret, though she supposed it was only a matter of time before things would come to a head.

Meanwhile, Betsy was becoming increasingly conflicted about the lively social life swirling around her. One day she wrote in her diary, "Worldly company, I think, materially injures; it excites a false stimulus, such as love of pomp, pride, vanity, jealousy, and ambition. . . . My mind feels very flat after this storm of pleasure."

A few pages later she wrote about how she was looking forward to a visit by Prince William Frederick of Gloucester, the king's nephew. But next she wrote,

> I have known my faults, and not corrected them and now I am determined I will once more try, with redoubled ardour, to overcome my wicked inclinations; I must not flirt; I must not ever be out of temper with the children; I must not contradict without cause; I must not mump [feel jealous] when my sisters are liked and I am not; I must not allow myself to be angry; . . . exaggerate; . . . give way to luxury; . . . be idle in mind.

Betsy tried to do all of these things, but it did not seem possible for her to change herself. She confessed to her journal, "I am at this present time in an odd state; I am like a ship put out to sea without a pilot; I feel my heart and mind so overburdened, I want someone to lean upon."

Despite her weekly Quaker meetings, Betsy did not think it was possible to lean on God. She felt she was closest to being a deist, someone who acknowledged there was a God somewhere out there in the universe but who believed that God did not concern Himself with the daily affairs of men. She outlined her thoughts in her diary:

> I have no more religion than that, and in the little I have I am not the least devotional. . . . My idea of religion is not that it should make us unfit for the duties of life like a nun who leaves them for prayer and thanksgiving; but I think it should stimulate and capacitate us to perform those duties properly.

Around and around Betsy went, like the soldiers who patrolled Norwich. Once she wanted to dance and sing the night away, and later she felt ashamed of her behavior and wrote, "I think I shall soon be rather religious because I have thought lately what a support it is through life; it seems so delightful to depend upon a superior power, for all that is good." But then she quickly talked herself out of it. "I fear being religious," she wrote, "in case I should become enthusiastic." Betsy dreaded that thought more than anything else. What could be worse, she wondered, than attending meetings constantly, dressing in old-fashioned clothes, and giving up everything that was bright and exciting in the world?

Yet Betsy also feared that her life would be over before she had accomplished anything worthwhile. "I am a bubble," she wrote, "without beauty of mind or person. I am a fool, I daily fall lower in my own estimation. . . . I am now seventeen and if some kind and great circumstance does not happen to me, I shall have my talents devoured by moth and rust."

What Betsy did not know was that a man from America was about to turn her world upside down.

Chapter 3

The Man from America

Betsy awoke on Sunday morning, February 4, 1798, with a stomachache. She watched as her sister Richenda drew back the drapes. Outside, elm branches swayed in the wind, and icicles hung from the cornice. Betsy wiggled farther under the down comforter. One glimpse out the window confirmed she should stay home beside the fire today. Her siblings might be corralled by their father into going to Goats, as the Gurney children referred to the Quaker meetinghouse on Goat Lane. However, Betsy knew that her father would not insist on her attending. She often used a poor night's sleep or some ache or pain to get out of her obligation to attend Sunday meetings.

Much to Betsy's surprise, this Sunday was different. Betsy sent Rachel down to tell their father that she would not be going to the meeting. Within minutes her father was standing at the bedroom door. "You must come," he said. "I have promised your Uncle Joseph that you will all be there."

"I'm too ill," Betsy said. "Besides, Uncle Joseph won't miss me. Everyone else will be there."

"That's not true," her father replied. "Uncle Joseph specifically asked me to make sure that you were coming. He thinks you will profit from hearing the speaker today."

Betsy wanted to roll her eyes, but that was something she never did in front of her father. *Nothing has ever happened at Goats that I could profit from,* she thought.

"Why must I go today, Father? The wind is howling and I slept poorly. I would prefer to stay indoors."

John Gurney walked over and stood beside his daughter's bed. "I know, I know, but the speaker is quite extraordinary. His name is William Savery, and he comes from America. He is one of the leading Quakers over there and is much sought after. He stands against slavery and has petitioned the United States Congress to have it abolished."

Betsy paid greater attention. She'd been interested in America ever since her mother had read to her about the revolution. Betsy and her sisters had even read Thomas Paine's *Common Sense* aloud to each other.

"And," her father continued, "he stands with the Indians. He was invited to watch over treaty negotiations with some tribal confederation to make sure the Indians were treated fairly."

"Oh," Betsy replied. "Under normal circumstances I should like to hear him, but I'm not well, Father. I am sure Kitty will tell me all about it when you return."

Betsy expected her father to leave it at that, but he persisted. "Your Uncle Joseph also said that William Savery was not always a Plain Quaker, as he is today. Once he was more modern, until he underwent a powerful inward transformation. He thought you should hear about that for yourself."

Betsy sighed. She did not want to leave her warm bed, but it was apparent her father was not about to give up. Besides, he asked so little of her that she felt obliged to make the effort and accompany the family to the meeting. "Very well, Father. If it means that much to you, I will come. But I hope we are able to leave straight after the meeting is over. I don't wish to linger."

"Fine," John replied. "I will leave you to dress."

An hour later the entire Gurney family entered the old Dutch-style Quaker meetinghouse. Betsy and her sisters went to the right, while her father and the two little boys, Joseph John and Daniel, turned to the left to find their seats among the menfolk. The two older boys, John and Sam, were away at boarding school.

Betsy had to squeeze past several women to find her seat in the family's pew. When she sat down, she looked around. It was astonishing. *There must be about two hundred people here,* she thought. Betsy had never seen Goats so full, or so colorful, for that matter. The place reminded her more of a playhouse than a Quaker meetinghouse. All sorts of modern Quakers, who seldom attended meetings, were there.

After everyone had found a seat, the meeting descended into silence. Betsy stared at the front platform, where several Quaker elders—including Uncle Joseph—sat flanking a middle-aged man, who Betsy assumed was William Savery. *I hope he speaks soon,* she thought. *Nothing would be more embarrassing than to have all these people come to hear him, and for him to sit there in silence for the entire meeting.* She knew this was a distinct possibility. She'd seen it happen before.

The meeting began in silence, and the minutes dragged on. Betsy looked down at her boots and admired the way they were polished to a high shine. *Surely,* she thought, *Mr. Savery will say something soon. Did he sail all the way across the Atlantic Ocean to sit in silence with us?*

People shuffled their feet and adjusted their clothing. Betsy watched the woman in front of her nervously wind her purse string around her fingers. Children whispered and giggled, and Betsy began to wish she had not come. Then, just when it felt to her like things were getting out of control, William Savery stood. He was taller than Betsy expected. He stared at the audience, and they stared back. An eternity seemed to pass between them. Betsy held her breath. Would he sit down again, or would he address the hall full of people?

"I am grieved by the gaiety I see in Norwich," William began in a soft but penetrating voice, "and I am especially grieved by what I see among the Friends here at Goat Lane."

Betsy felt herself blush. She adjusted her blue skirt so that it covered her boots.

"What has become of true religion?" William went on. "That is a question every man, woman, and child must answer in their own heart. What dost thou say? Art thou walking the paths of virtue or hast thou abandoned them for the way of selfishness, indifference, and greed?"

William then went on to talk about how Jesus encouraged His followers to lay up treasure for themselves in heaven, but that many Friends today were more interested in laying up earthly treasures. "Dost thou think thee will live forever?" he asked. "Have thine ancestors lived forever? Are they among us? Man's life on earth is fleeting—over in the blink of an eye—what makes thee think otherwise?"

Betsy's mind wandered to the graveyard where her mother lay buried. *Mr. Savery is right,* she thought. *No one is going to live forever. One day I will stand before the judgment seat of Christ. What shall I say to Him? What will I bring to Him?*

Then abruptly, William finished speaking and sat down. Betsy looked around. No one moved. As she wiped tears from her eyes, she noticed that she wasn't the only one doing so. And then everyone stood up. The meeting was over, and William Savery walked off the platform. Much to her surprise, Betsy felt deflated. She could have listened to the man speak all day.

"Let's get out of here before we bump into Uncle Joseph," Betsy heard Richenda say.

Betsy dragged her feet. For once she wanted to see her uncle, if only to ask him where Mr. Savery was speaking next.

As it turned out, Uncle Joseph and his wife, Jane, had invited the Plain Quakers at the meeting to dine at their home with William Savery. "Wouldst thou like to join us, Betsy?" her uncle asked, using Plain Quaker language.

Betsy nodded. "I should like that very much," she said, avoiding the glances of her sisters. She knew they would laugh at her wanting to hear more from a Plain Quaker, but something irresistible about William Savery drew her in.

"Thou canst ride home with me, and then back to Gildencroft for the afternoon meeting if thou likest."

As Betsy joined her uncle and aunt in their coach, she watched her father, sisters, and brothers climb into theirs. It was a strange moment. Somehow she knew she was setting off on a different path, one they would not understand.

Lunch, as she expected, was a grand affair. The food itself was plain—roast pork, pumpkin soup, and bread—but the surroundings were opulent. Uncle Joseph and his wife now lived in the Gurney family's ancestral home of Keswick Hall just a few miles from Earlham. Although Betsy had visited the place many times, this time she felt like a stranger. She wanted so desperately to ask William Savery some questions, but instead she shrunk into the shadows, certain he would not notice her.

When lunch was over, Uncle Joseph came to his niece. "Betsy, wouldst thou like to speak privately with Mr. Savery?"

Betsy nodded, not trusting herself to speak.

"Very well. Thou and he shall ride together in my coach back to town. Does that please thee?"

"Yes, Uncle," Betsy replied, her heart racing. Then she frowned. Why did she care so much about this man and his message? Was his message really all that different from anything she'd heard a hundred—no, a thousand—times before at Goats? Betsy was not sure, but something in what he said struck her differently.

Sure enough, Betsy found herself alone with the famous American. She wanted to pour out her heart to him, to ask him a million questions, but she didn't. Instead a few attempts were made at conversation, followed by long silences. Betsy almost wished that she hadn't come, but somewhere deep inside, her heart was stirred.

The coach was headed for Gildencroft, the second and much larger Quaker meetinghouse in Norwich. As it rounded Saint Crispin's Road, Betsy gasped. The area was clogged with carriages and horses. Unlike the morning meeting at Goats, this meeting was open to the public. Over two thousand people had turned out to hear William Savery speak.

Betsy found herself a seat in the meetinghouse and waited to hear what William would say this time. William's message was similar to the one he delivered in the morning, although it was not directed just to Friends. He pointed out that any society that did not hold firm to the foundations of the Christian faith was liable to decay morally and spiritually and that the greatest foundation of the Christian faith was to promote peace on earth and goodwill toward all people. He heaped scorn upon the notion that countries that declared themselves to be Christian would delight in war or even think it acceptable to thank God for victory over an enemy.

Something about what William said and the way he said it deeply touched Betsy. On the way home in the family's carriage Betsy could not stop weeping. She knew her sisters were watching her, but she couldn't stop.

That evening Betsy wrote in her journal,

> I have had a faint light spread over my mind; at least, I believe it is something of that kind, owing to having been much with and having heard much excellence from one who appears to me to be a true Christian, it has caused me to feel a little religion. My imagination has been worked upon, and I fear that what I have felt will go off. . . . I wish the state of enthusiasm I am now in may last, for today I have felt there is a God, I have been devotional, and my mind has been led away from the follies that it is mostly wrapped up in.

A week later Betsy was less sure about what she had experienced in William's meeting. She wrote,

> Today I have felt all my old irreligious feelings. My object shall be to search, try to do right,

> and if I am mistaken, it is not my fault, but the state I am now in makes it difficult to act. What little religion I have felt has been owing to my giving way quietly and humbly to my feelings: but the more I reason upon it the more I get into a labyrinth of uncertainty, and my mind is so much inclined to both skepticism and enthusiasm, that if I argue and doubt, I shall be a total skeptic; if, on the contrary I give way to it, and, as it were, wait for religion, I may be led away.

Now Betsy did not know what to do. She felt torn between two worlds—the world of pleasure and partying and the world of Christian faith and a life of obedience to God. She wondered how she would ever make up her mind one way or the other.

A week later she had an answer. She would travel to London once again and investigate both options. There she could stay with her wealthy relatives and at the same time attend Quaker meetings where William and other Americans from his group were speaking. Betsy made up her mind. She would not return to Earlham Hall until she had figured out which direction she should go.

Chapter 4

What She Had Been Waiting For

Elizabeth Gurney had made the 150-mile journey from Earlham Hall to London only once before as a young girl. On that trip she had been severely depressed and stayed within the confines of her relatives' home in London, only venturing out to see her doctor. This time she anticipated a very different experience. Her father and a lady's maid named Joan accompanied her on the journey south from Norwich. So far the trip had been uneventful. The travelers had set out soon after sunrise and stopped at Attleborough to exchange their horses for post-horses. Post-horses were animals hired from the postmaster to pull a carriage to the next stop or post house. John Gurney paid to have his horses stalled and fed in Attleborough until he picked them up on his return journey to Norwich.

The next leg of the trip was more harrowing. Betsy's father hired an armed postilion, a rider who sat atop the leading horse on the left side and kept a lookout for highwaymen or other forms of trouble. Betsy felt nervous as she gazed out the carriage window. Several other horse-drawn carriages passed them going the opposite direction, but the Gurney carriage was obviously the most luxurious of them all. It was well sprung and had polished brass door handles. The outside was lacquered to a high sheen while the inside was trimmed with a tan-colored silk lining. Betsy was sure their carriage would be an obvious target for robbers. She pulled the sheepskin rug tight around her and watched out the window.

The travelers broke the journey at White Hart Inn in Thetford, thirty miles from home. Betsy and her father dined together in the parlor before retiring to bed. The next morning they were up early and on their way before the frost had melted. Through towns and villages the coach wound its way, the postilion all the time watchful for any sign of an ambush. The stretch of the journey across New Market Heath left Betsy a nervous wreck. She wished some of her sisters had come with her, but then she remembered why she was undertaking the journey—to make up her own mind about her future.

Betsy was relieved when they arrived in London safe and sound, though her nerves were on edge and she retired early to bed. She awoke the next morning determined to make the most of her visit. Her father left for Norwich later that morning, leaving Betsy and Joan alone with the Barclay clan in their mansion in Clapham.

And what a clan it was. Uncle David Barclay, Betsy's mother's uncle, was the co-owner of the brewery Barclay Perkins and Company. He explained to Betsy how, with the addition of a new Boulton and Watt steam engine to help mechanize production, he intended to turn the company into the largest brewery in the world.

Betsy had come expecting to experience two Londons, the glittering world of the Barclays and the sober and pious world inside the Quaker meetinghouses where William Savery preached and taught. She was not disappointed. From the day she arrived, her second cousins drew her into their social whirl. They attended plays at the Drury Lane Theatre, spent evenings at the Royal Opera on Bow Street, and took trips to waxworks, puppet shows, and horticultural exhibitions.

Betsy also visited her friend Amelia Alderson, who was preparing to marry the famous painter John Opie. Amelia introduced Betsy to a glamorous new set of friends, who included art patrons, artists, writers, and musicians. One night they attended a play where Betsy sat alongside the Prince of Wales. Betsy was particularly made up for the occasion, having borrowed Amelia's makeup and hairdresser. It felt strange and unnatural to her, and she complained to Amelia that she felt like a pet monkey with her hair piled high on her head, a hairstyle that took three hours to complete and half that time again to dismantle.

In the midst of this social whirl, Betsy kept the promise to herself to attend as many local Quaker meetings as she could. On Sundays she followed

William Savery from meetinghouse to meetinghouse and also had several private meetings with him. When she was with William, she was instantly drawn back into his world—the world of faith in God and good works—but it was hard to keep that reality alive when she returned to her uncle's house.

Betsy's trip to London lasted six weeks, and in early April her father arrived to take her home. The trip home was much more pleasant. The days were getting longer, and spring was in the air. Daffodils and crocuses dotted the hillsides. Bright green grass sprouted through the mud, and lambs and calves frolicked in the sunlight.

As she traveled back north, Betsy tried to sort through her London experiences. She had enjoyed her times with William Savery and the other Plain Quakers, but she had also been elated when she sat near the Prince of Wales. Now she had to decide which path to follow. As she struggled with this, she wrote in her journal,

> I must look to One higher than he [William Savery]; and if I feel my own soul satisfied I need not fear. Look up to true religion as the very first of blessings, cherish it, nourish and let it flourish and bloom in my heart; it wants taking care of, it is difficult to obtain. I must not despair or grow skeptical, if I do not always feel religious. I felt God as it were and I must seek to find him again.

Slowly and deliberately Betsy began to change her behavior. She did not want to go so far as to dress like a Plain Quaker, but she did wear simpler clothes. She also promised to dance and sing less and spend more time at Friends meetings.

All of this caused a lot of tension in the Gurney household. Betsy's father begged her not to become extreme and then forbade her to visit a dying man in the village for whom she was praying and to whom she was reading the Bible. Rachel, her closest sister, was chosen by her siblings to deliver a message to Betsy. "We all feel the same way. All seven of us sisters have always been in agreement, and now you are separating yourself from the rest of us. It is very grieving."

Betsy did not want to upset her sisters, but she felt compelled to press on. This was partly because of the recurring dream she'd had since her mother's death. Until returning from London, over and over Betsy had had the same terrifying dream of being dragged under the waves. But when she got home and set her course on faith in God, the dream stopped. Betsy was relieved to be able to go to bed without dreading the dream.

When Betsy was a child still living in Norwich at her grandmother's house, she had watched her mother and grandmother take food to poor people, but things were somehow different living on a sprawling country estate. If poor people begged at the kitchen door, Betsy was not aware of it. Nor did she walk past the washerwoman's cottage and peek in to see if she had bedding or not. Betsy set out to investigate the lives of the poor people who worked around the estate. She soon found plenty of needs, and with her allowance she bought cotton and sewed a dress for a new mother, bought nine shillings' worth of bedding for another, and gave a young boy half a crown so he could attend school.

Betsy felt the most satisfaction from giving the last gift. She knew that reading and writing were keys to getting along in life, and just as important was being able to read the Bible for oneself. Suddenly Betsy's mind ran wild with possibilities. What if all the boys and girls in the area could learn to read and write? Was that something she could help with?

To accomplish such a goal, Betsy knew she needed to divide the task into small steps. She decided to start with just one boy. She chose Billy Coslington, whose mother was a widow. Each Sunday night she visited the Coslingtons' cottage and helped Billy sound out words. Billy was a good student, and before long he could read simple sentences. Betsy was elated. She invited another boy to join her, and then another.

In July a man from London arrived at Earlham Hall—twenty-one-year-old Joseph Fry. Joseph had attended boarding school with Betsy's brother John, and Betsy had been introduced to him while she was in London. Even so, she was surprised to see him galloping up the long, curved driveway to the house. She wondered what he wanted. Joseph came from a Plain Quaker family who were bankers as well as tea and spice importers. His uncle, whom he was named after, was the owner of the Fry Chocolate Company. Like Betsy's Barclay relatives, Joseph's uncle had made a lot of money by using the latest Boulton and Watt steam engine to mechanize the process of grinding the cocoa beans to speed along the production of the chocolate.

Joseph stayed at Earlham Hall for several days, and Betsy spent a lot of time studying him. For all his family's wealth and connections, Joseph seemed to her to be lacking in elegance and polish.

As Joseph rode away after his stay, John Gurney came up with a novel idea. He asked his seven daughters if they would like to accompany him on a trip to see Wales and southwest England. By now the two youngest boys were away at boarding school. The girls all agreed to the trip, and they set out with their father on July 21, 1798, with two carriages—a chariot and a chaise. Their first stop was London, where they stayed with their Barclay relatives. Betsy was delighted to find that William Savery's ship had been delayed and that he was still in London. She and her entire family attended his farewell meeting, and Betsy gave him a kid-leather pocketbook as a parting gift.

From London the seven sisters and their father traveled south, touring through southwest England before venturing into Wales. Most of the time other wealthy Quaker families hosted the Gurneys and their servants, and many of these other Quaker families were related to them in some way.

Betsy enjoyed parts of the three-month trip, but her heart was back in Earlham with the boys she had been teaching to read. She wondered if they were still practicing their words or if they had forgotten what she had taught them. There were trials along the way too. The Gurney girls were invited to many dances, about which Betsy felt conflicted. Betsy felt out of place at such events, but she did not want to cause a rift in the family. Whenever possible she attended Quaker meetings, but her sisters made fun of her for doing so. By the time they arrived in Shropshire on the last leg of their journey, Betsy was tired and depressed. She did not know what to do.

In Shropshire the Gurneys stayed at Dale House in Coalbrookdale. In 1707, Abraham Darby, a Quaker and brass manufacturer, had moved from Bristol to Coalbrookdale, where he reopened a derelict blast furnace and set up an iron foundry. In the process of doing this, Darby devised an innovative new way to smelt iron, allowing for the continuous casting of cast iron goods rather than their being cast individually. This approach both sped up and reduced the cost of working with cast iron. By 1798 Darby's invention was being widely used in foundries across England. Twenty years earlier Abraham Darby III had been involved in casting the iron for and helping to build the world's first iron bridge across the nearby Severn River. Now four women—three widows and a granddaughter of Abraham Darby—ran the company, and the Gurneys stayed with them. While in Coalbrookdale Betsy enjoyed a walk across the impressive iron bridge over the Severn and visited the Darbys' foundry to see the iron being smelted.

On the morning of September 3, during the Gurneys' stay in Coalbrookdale, Betsy awoke early and went downstairs to see if anyone else was up. She found one of the widows, Deborah Darby, alone in the dining room. Deborah asked Betsy to join her for breakfast. Deborah Darby was a Quaker legend, and Betsy felt nervous being alone in her presence. Several years before, Deborah had sailed to America, where she visited New York and Pennsylvania to preach against slavery. She even crossed the Allegheny Mountains with a wagon train to preach in the small, isolated settlements on the American frontier.

Deborah and Betsy made small talk as they ate. After a servant cleared away the dishes, the room fell silent. Betsy could feel her heart thumping. She clasped her hands together nervously under the table. After several minutes Deborah cleared her throat and looked at Betsy. "God will visit us all," she said. "God, who is father to the fatherless, and mother to the motherless. You are sick of the world, so you look higher, and you who are to be dedicated to God will have peace in this world and glory everlasting in the world to come."

Betsy trembled at these words. For the rest of the day she thought about what Deborah had said to her. Betsy's cousin Priscilla Gurney also lived in Coalbrookdale, and Betsy discussed Deborah's words with her. Much to Betsy's relief, Priscilla understood her situation. By evening, Betsy had come to a stunning conclusion, which she recorded in her diary. "A Plain Friend I believe I must be."

Betsy would no longer be concerned about dancing or not dancing, how elaborately to do her hair, or what to wear. She knew she would spend the rest of her life as a Plain Quaker. She did not speak to anyone in her family about her decision. In his or her own way, each member of her family had expressed frustrations and concerns about Betsy's increasing enthusiasm for religion, but now she didn't care.

The following night after dinner, Priscilla invited Betsy to join the Plain Quaker women in the parlor. Once more the women sat in silence. Then Deborah Darby spoke up. "You will be a light to the blind, speech to the dumb, and feet to the lame," she said to Betsy. Silence again fell over the group. Something deep inside Betsy stirred. This was what she had been waiting for all along—something to do for God and for her fellow man.

Chapter 5

A New Life

On the trip back to the Earlham estate during the final leg of the Gurney family's tour of southwest England and Wales, Betsy formed a plan. She wanted to transform herself into a Plain Quaker, which she thought would eliminate a number of unnecessary decisions from her life. She knew that once she donned Quaker dress—for a woman a plain-colored dress with a white kerchief folded into the neckline and a white bonnet—people would no longer expect her to partake in many activities. They wouldn't ask her to dance or attend operas or spend the evening playing cards. Plain Quakers simply did not do such things.

Over the next few months, Betsy made the transition to become a Plain Quaker. Some parts of the change, such as wearing Quaker dress, seemed easy, though she struggled to hide her long, flaxen hair beneath the bonnet. Other things took a while to get used to, such as saying *thou* and *thee* to her family and the servants. Yet as embarrassing as this was at first, she overcame it. And for the first time in her life, Betsy enjoyed going to Quaker meetings, where she soon made friends with some of the other Plain Friends, many of whom she and her sisters had previously mocked.

Along with the outward changes, Betsy found a new, inner strength. She took more poor boys and girls under her care to teach them to read and write. Her sisters found it hard to believe she would willingly spend time with the children, whom they referred to as "Betsy's imps," but for once Betsy did not care. She conducted her classes in the laundry room, and before long, seventy children were taking part.

Betsy knew that her father had been concerned about her becoming a Plain Quaker, but she felt some of his anxieties were laid to rest when he came to visit her class one day. "You were born to serve others," he told Betsy, "and I will help you in any way I can."

Betsy was relieved. She thought her father finally understood what really made his third daughter happy. She also began to expand her services, which soon included teaching the girls to sew and delivering baskets of food to the poorest families in the area.

All was going well for Betsy when Joseph Fry appeared at Earlham Hall for a second and then a third time. Betsy soon realized that he was not as interested in visiting her brother John as he was in courting her. She did not know what to make of Joseph. Sometimes she liked being around him; other times she found him clingy and overbearing.

Betsy also was concerned about how getting married would affect the rest of the family. Her sister Kitty, who had taken on the role of mother to them all, had given up any hope of marrying, and Rachel swore that if she could not marry Henry Enfield, a non-Quaker, she would remain single. This meant that Betsy would be the first daughter in the family to marry and move away from Earlham—all the way to London. Joseph had informed Betsy that if they married, his older brother William and his wife, Eliza, would move out of Mildred's Court, the Fry home on Poultry, a street in central London, so that he and Betsy could use it. Betsy could not imagine being cooped up in a house in noisy, smoky London when she had been raised in the lovely countryside around Norwich.

The other thing that concerned Betsy was her role as a Christian wife and possibly a mother. She loved teaching her "imps" and wanted to find some way to continue that work. Was it possible to be a wife and mother and a worker among the poor? She discussed the matter with Joseph, who assured her that if she married him he would support whatever kind of work she wanted to do. Still, Betsy could not make up her mind.

On his fourth visit to Earlham, on May 24, 1800, Joseph appeared to Betsy to have had enough of wooing her. He gave her an ultimatum: either Betsy agreed to marry him or he would never bother her again. He told her that the next morning he would leave a gold watch on the seat in the rose garden. If she picked up the watch, it would be a sign that she would have him as a husband. If she left it on the seat, he would leave that afternoon and never return.

The following morning Betsy stood and stared at the gold watch. Should she pick it up and signal the beginning of a new life for herself in London, or should she leave it where it was and stay at Earlham with her sisters and brothers? Quietly Betsy stooped down and picked up the watch. She would marry Joseph Fry, and together they would find a way to serve God. In her journal she wrote, "My feelings toward Joseph are so calm and pleasant, and I can look forward with so much cheerfulness to a connection with him."

The wedding of Elizabeth Gurney and Joseph Fry took place on Sunday, August 19, 1800, at the meetinghouse on Goat Lane. Betsy wore her Plain Quaker clothes, while all of her sisters had pretty new dresses made for the occasion.

Holding her father's arm, Betsy, followed by her sisters and brothers, entered the hushed meetinghouse. She sat beside her father and Kitty on a bench at the front, facing the congregation. Joseph sat with his family on another bench, also facing the congregation. After a few moments of solemn silence, Joseph stood, walked over to Betsy, and took her by the hand. Betsy rose, and the couple stood side by side. "In the presence of the Lord and this assembly," Joseph began hastily, "I take this my friend, Elizabeth Gurney, to be my wife, promising by divine assistance to be unto her a loving and faithful husband until it shall please the Lord by death to separate us."

When Joseph had spoken, it was Betsy's turn to speak. "Friends, in the presence of the Lord and of this assembly, I take this my friend, Joseph Fry, to be my husband, promising through divine assistance to be unto him a loving and faithful wife until it shall please the Lord by death to separate us."

With that Betsy and Joseph were married.

Betsy's brother John and one of her cousins carried a small table to the front of the meetinghouse. On it lay the wedding certificate with two pens and an inkwell. First Joseph and then Betsy dipped their pens in ink and signed their names to the certificate. Then Betsy's uncle Joseph picked up the wedding certificate and, as was customary among the Quakers, read it aloud. This was followed by an hour of prayer for the newlyweds, and then Joseph led Betsy, now Mrs. Elizabeth Fry, from the meetinghouse.

When they reached London, the couple took up residence in Mildred's Court. Betsy had assumed that her new life in London would be much the same as it had been in Earlham, except for the lack of large grounds to ride and walk on. It took her only half a day to realize how wrong she'd been.

Joseph's older brother William and his wife, Eliza, who had previously lived in the house, had moved in with Joseph's parents at the Plashet estate, the Frys' large country home in East Ham. Now that he was married, Joseph was to take over the daily running of the family's tea and spice business, receiving boxes and boxes of spices and tea that arrived from the Near and Far East on the tall-masted ships that docked along the Thames River. He then warehoused the boxes in the building next to Mildred's Court, from where they would be distributed throughout England. Joseph was also involved with his father and brother in running the various banking services that W. S. Fry & Sons provided.

But when Betsy arrived at her new home in London, her sister-in-law, Eliza, was still in the process of moving her belongings out. Boxes and pieces of furniture were everywhere. Chaos was the only word Betsy could think of to describe the state of her new home. And it did not look like the situation would improve anytime soon. Both William and Eliza still treated the house as if they lived there, arriving at all hours of the day or night, ordering the servants to make them meals, or taking naps in any room they chose. Betsy tried hard to remain pleasant and welcoming, but she longed to put her new house in order.

To make matters worse, Mildred's Court was located just a few hundred yards from the Bank of England and was a natural stopping-off place for the many wealthy Quakers who came to do business in the capital city. To Betsy's surprise, Sunday proved to be the busiest day of the week for her. The Frys attended the meetinghouse on Gracechurch Street, a very old Quaker meetinghouse and just a short distance from Mildred's Court. Betsy soon learned that just about everyone who attended the meetinghouse assumed they had an open invitation to Sunday lunch at Mildred's Court.

Besides this, Betsy inherited the task of hosting visiting Quakers. Her first guest was George Dilwyn from Philadelphia in the United States. He arrived soon after she had settled in and announced that he would be staying for six weeks. In her journal, Betsy confided that she found him quite a trial. His table manners were sloppy, and he made pointed comments about her beautiful home. Betsy found this particularly annoying, since Mr. Dilwyn was quite happy to stay in it with them.

At Christmas the entire Fry family descended on Mildred's Court. They inspected every room of the house, offering their opinions on how Betsy had placed her furniture and how fashionable the drapes were. This angered Betsy. It seemed that no matter how hard she tried, she could not please everyone. Her sisters complained she was too plain and went to too many meetings, while her in-laws found her house too fancy, and even Joseph had to talk to her about how her manners were too refined.

Despite it all, Betsy kept going. When she found the courage to speak more bluntly to her brother-in-law, William, she instantly regretted it. Then, when she gave the footman firm orders which he did not carry out correctly, she failed to confront and correct him. Most of all, Betsy tried to prepare herself for the dreaded yearly meeting that was coming up in May. Just the thought of the event made her want to flee back to Earlham. The yearly meeting gathered

Quakers from around the country for two weeks to discuss spiritual issues and various practical matters. The meetings were held in the nearby Devonshire House building, and it had become Fry tradition that Mildred's Court be an open house during the time of the yearly meeting for visiting Quakers to come and eat and rest at will. Betsy was told that it was not unusual for forty or even sixty people to show up for dinner. Not only would she be the hostess, but also she would need to oversee the house staff as they prepared endless meals and kept the house as clean and organized as possible. She would also be expected to attend the yearly meetings herself.

By the time May and the yearly meeting arrived, Betsy was six months pregnant, with the baby due in August on or near her first wedding anniversary. Yet being pregnant was no excuse to shirk her responsibilities as hostess and house manager. Betsy felt overwhelmed at the task ahead. She longed for those simple days when she had listened with enthusiasm to William Savery preach. How long ago that seemed now. As she sat on the hard wooden seat at the meetings, her back aching from the pregnancy, all she could think of was how many people would soon walk from the meeting hall at Devonshire House to Mildred's Court to indulge in her hospitality.

Betsy was soon busier than ever, overseeing feeding the constant flow of Quaker visitors to Mildred's Court and attending meetings herself. To her dismay, Betsy discovered that after eating, her Quaker guests would usually decide to take a nap.

Every horizontal surface in the house would soon have someone lying on it as the house vibrated with the sound of snoring. On top of all this, Betsy found many of the meetings she attended disappointing and trivial. All sorts of minor topics were being debated as if they would save the world. The size of a man's hat brim was discussed, as was the spacing of the benches in the meetinghouse. One particularly long meeting lasted four hours, during which Betsy sat dutifully before returning home to welcome the throng. It was difficult to drag herself back to the meetings day after day. Betsy wrote in her journal, "The state of deadness of religion has been my recent experience." She flashed back to Deborah Darby's words to her in Coalbrookdale that she would be a light to the blind and feet to the lame. How unlikely that seemed to her now.

As far as Betsy was concerned, there was really only one bright spot to the entire yearly meeting, and that was a visit to the Free School on Borough Road in George's Field. One of the visitors to the meetings was Joseph Lancaster, who had started a school for boys near the Thames River. Joseph invited anyone who was interested to come and tour the facility. As tired as she was, Betsy jumped at the opportunity to see someone doing something other than just talking. She joined five other Quakers in a carriage that took them to the school. Joseph Lancaster, a stocky, dark-haired man, met them at the gate. Betsy judged him to be about her age.

"The school is only a year old. I hope thou wilt bear that in mind," Joseph said as he helped Betsy from the carriage. "The whole aim of it is to give poor boys, and hopefully girls soon, the chance to read and write."

"How are thee doing that?" an older Friend asked.

"Those who can pay, I charge one guinea a year per student, and the rest are quietly excused from payment. It is a private matter between us, and no one else knows who is a free pupil and who is not. I do not have enough money for next year yet, but if I am a faithful steward, I believe God will supply our needs. I have devised some new methods to keep down the cost of educating each boy."

"How so?" Betsy asked as she walked up the cobblestone path toward the schoolhouse.

"I use polished slates and pencils for the older children and sand trays in which the younger boys practice their spelling and writing. They write with a stick and then smooth the sand back and try again. It is very economical. In other schools each child has his own workbook, but I've had large charts of each page printed and pasted to wooden boards so that one chart can be used hundreds of times. The only ongoing expense is pencils for the slates. But the heart of my method relies on the economy of teachers. I have devised a new system whereby one teacher—such as myself—can teach a thousand students."

Betsy frowned. She thought back to her seventy or so "imps" in the laundry room at Earlham. It had been difficult enough attending to and teaching that number of children. How could Joseph possibly keep any sense of discipline with many times the number of students? Surely he was exaggerating. It was not possible to teach that many children at once.

A few minutes later Betsy found herself standing in a large, rectangular room with sloping floors. The older children were at the back, and the younger ones were closer to the front.

"That's where I stand, on that platform where everyone can see me," Joseph explained. "But I'm just a part of a large system run by monitors, older boys who can read and write. I instruct them every morning first thing, and then they spend the rest of the day instructing others. Each boy is assessed by me and put into a group of boys who know as much as he does, and they are assigned a monitor. It's the monitor's job to take them through a set of charts until they know them. Then each lad is tested, and if he knows the work, he goes up to the next bench and learns from a new monitor."

"How many scholars dost thou currently have?" Betsy asked.

"About three hundred now, but there is room for many more," he said, his eyes shining. "I wish to expand until every boy and girl in England has the opportunity to learn to read and write. The fact that they do not have that opportunity is a national evil and requires a national remedy. It can no longer be delayed. We need to expand our minds, to free them from every narrow principle and unite as Christians for the common public good."

Betsy felt like applauding. How refreshing it was to hear a fellow Quaker talking about uniting with other Christians and actually getting something done. Right then and there she decided she would do whatever possible to help Joseph.

Once the yearly meeting was over, Betsy set two goals for herself. The first was to prepare for the birth of her baby, due mid-August, and the second was to raise money for the Free School. By August she had raised twenty-six guineas for Joseph Lancaster, enough to ensure his school continued. Now she awaited the birth.

Two of Betsy's sisters, Rachel and Hannah, arrived in London from Earlham to help her with the delivery, but it was still a terrifying prospect, especially when Betsy learned that one of her old friends from Norwich had died giving birth to her first child. The risks were real, and as she waited to give birth, Betsy tried hard to remind herself how blessed she was to be wealthy enough to have a doctor on hand if anything went wrong.

Chapter 6

Up and Down

On August 22, 1801, just three days after her and Joseph's first wedding anniversary, Betsy gave birth to a baby girl. The labor was long and difficult, but the child, whom they named Katherine, arrived pink and healthy. Betsy held the newborn in her arms and looked up at Joseph, who was obviously delighted to have a daughter. Betsy, however, was too exhausted to care.

Betsy forced a smile as she looked at her new daughter. She tried hard to appear happy, but inside she felt tired and depressed. Having a baby only seemed to add to her burden. Each time Katherine cried, Betsy was concerned that her daughter might have one of the many deadly diseases that killed about 30 percent of babies born in London. And holding the baby made her think of her mother. The last baby her mother had cared for was Daniel, born ten years before. Betsy remembered her mother as being kind and gentle as she looked after Betsy's newly arrived little brother. But as she stared at her own child, who bore the same name as her mother, waves of sadness rolled over her. Betsy stayed in bed and had Katherine brought to her when the baby needed to be nursed.

In the meantime, a military struggle had been going on between France and Great Britain following the French Revolution. The Treaty of Amiens, signed in March 1802, was intended to end the struggle between the two nations. Even the celebration in the streets of London following the signing of the treaty could not coax Betsy from her bedroom. In fact, Betsy found the celebration to be an annoyance, and it was hard for her to sleep with so much noise outside.

As time passed, Betsy slowly began to interact again with the world. She got out of bed and stood at the window, staring out at the courtyard. She noticed the bells of Saint Mildred's Church as they rang at various times throughout the day and the sparrows that lined up on the high wall.

As Betsy turned her attention to the future, she recalled a discussion she'd heard about vaccinating against smallpox, one of the most dreaded diseases at the time. Smallpox killed about 20 percent of the population of England, with a high proportion of deaths being among babies and young children. Just eight years before, an English physician named Edward Jenner had scraped the pus from a cowpox blister into the arm of an eight-year-old boy. The boy quickly contracted cowpox, a disease that did not normally kill anyone. Dr. Jenner then set out to prove that once the boy had cowpox, he would be immune to, that is, unable to contract, smallpox. His findings seemed clear—inoculating with cowpox as a vaccine would stop the spread of smallpox.

Despite Dr. Jenner's conclusions, many people believed it was ill-advised to try such a risky treatment on a perfectly healthy child. After studying the matter carefully and speaking to her doctor about it, Betsy arrived at the decision to have Kitty, as baby Katherine was called, vaccinated. She watched as the doctor scratched Kitty deep between the thumb and forefinger of her right hand. Betsy calmed the now-crying child as the doctor then rubbed pustules into the scratch, immunizing Kitty against smallpox. Kitty ran a high fever after the inoculation, but she soon recovered.

Following Kitty's inoculation, Betsy felt well enough to visit Earlham with her new daughter. She walked on the estate grounds and left her sisters to dote over Kitty. While she was at Earlham, her father's second cousin, Bartlett Gurney, died childless. He had owned the large and well-respected Gurney Bank in Norwich, which he had inherited from his father and grandfather. Bartlett named Betsy's father and his brother Richard as his heirs. Betsy's father and uncle took over the banking business. John, Betsy's oldest brother, joined the two men, and it was agreed that Betsy's younger brother Sam would move to London to live with the Frys and learn what he could about bookkeeping and banking at Fry's Bank.

In March 1803 Betsy gave birth to a second daughter, whom she and Joseph named Rachel. Once again, following the birth, Betsy plunged into a deep depression. Her condition was not helped when in May 1803 Great Britain once again went to war with France. Despite the jubilation following the Treaty of Amiens the year before, the peace between the two nations had not lasted.

When Betsy heard that her mother-in-law was sick, she rallied herself. She traveled to East Ham with her two small children in tow and found renewed energy in nursing her mother-in-law, whom everyone referred to as Mother Fry. Betsy enjoyed trying to make Mother Fry comfortable and figuring out the exact effect of the various remedies the doctor tried.

All this led Betsy to think about what she really enjoyed doing in life. She wrote a list of the things she was doing at those times when she had felt truly alive. Only four things were on the list—teaching her imps, visiting poor families around Earlham, raising subscriptions for the Free School, and nursing her mother-in-law. Betsy pondered what these things had in common. The answer seemed fairly obvious: each one involved being useful and helping someone in need. With a streak of insight, Betsy realized that that was what she would have to do to be happy. After returning to London, as she looked out the window of Mildred's Court one day, she realized that just yards from the house were alleyways that led to hovels and people who could benefit from all that Betsy had to offer.

Betsy got up, reached for her bonnet, and left the house. Located in the heart of London, Mildred's Court was surrounded by many fine buildings. The Lord Mayor's Mansion House was to the left, the Royal Exchange was across the street, and builders were hard at work building a bigger and better structure to house the Bank of England. Shops lined the streets where people milled as they purchased all kinds of merchandise. Betsy walked past all of this and turned into an alley that led north. Soon she had left the grand buildings and shops behind and found herself in a maze of twisting alleyways lined with dilapidated tenements. Grubby children played in the filth of the alleys while men crouched in doorways and at corners drinking or arguing or just looking dully into the distance. Tattered clothing hung from makeshift clotheslines. Dogs and pigs rummaged through the trash strewn about. At first Betsy felt scared by the grim sight. She feared that everyone was watching her and that she might be attacked and robbed at any moment. She calmed her fears by reminding herself that she had asked God for His protection.

Slowly, as time passed, Betsy began to relax and stopped to talk to women as they hung laundry and tended unruly children. Despite the squalid conditions these people lived in, Betsy reminded herself that they were human beings in need of both God's love and compassion and the help of other humans. Several hours had passed before Betsy made it back to Mildred's Court.

That night Betsy confided in her diary, "I felt quite in my element serving the poor, and although I was much tired from looking about, it gave me much pleasure. It is an occupation my nature is so fond of. I wish not to take merit to myself beyond my desert, but it brings satisfaction with it more than most things."

A week later Betsy was appointed by the Quakers from her meetinghouse to oversee an inheritance from one of the group's members. The money was bequeathed to help the poor, and it was Betsy's job to visit and advise the orphans and widows who were to receive it. Betsy took this as a sign she was moving in the right direction. Over the next year she spent many afternoons walking in the back alleys near her home. She became familiar with the poorest people: the five-year-old chimney sweeps, the little girls selling posies in the street, the pickpockets, the men who had no work, the bedraggled women trying to scrape together scraps of food to feed their children. She sewed clothes for new babies, bought food for the starving, and sent her doctor to visit the dying.

As the New Year of 1804 dawned, things did not start well. Not only was Betsy midway through another difficult pregnancy, her third, but also Mother Fry's health had deteriorated and Betsy once more took on the job of nursing her. Despite Betsy's best efforts, her mother-in-law died in March 1804. Four months later, in July, Betsy gave birth to another child, her first son, whom they named John after her father and oldest brother.

Once again following the birth, Betsy fell into depression, and she began to wonder whether her life was worth living. At the same time, Joseph was feeling liberated by the death of his mother. He no longer attended Quaker meetings as often as Betsy thought he should, and he started playing chess, singing, and playing the piano. Betsy's sisters were delighted that their brother-in-law was becoming more like them, but Betsy was mortified. She was haunted by the idea that she might have done something to cause her husband to turn away from the strict path they had previously walked together.

Although Betsy longed to be useful to the poor, she found her life taken up with managing her household and caring for three small children. None of the children were very well behaved, and her sisters dubbed them "Betsy's brats." A cousin even came to the house to investigate just how badly the two older girls behaved at home. This was humiliating for Betsy, who reminded herself that she needed all the help and advice she could get in order to raise her children properly.

Despite her unruly children, Betsy pressed on trying to do what she could to help the poor and needy in London. Like everyone else in Great Britain, she was delighted when the news reached England on November 5, 1805, of the British navy's great victory over a combined French and Spanish naval force. The battle had been fought on October 21, 1805, off the southwest coast of Spain, just west of Cape Trafalgar. Twenty-seven British naval ships led by Admiral Lord Nelson aboard HMS *Victory* had engaged and defeated thirty-three French and Spanish naval ships, sinking twenty-two French and Spanish warships without the loss of a single British vessel. It was a proud day for Great Britain, but news of the naval victory was tempered by the fact that Admiral Nelson had been killed in the battle. Although it was a triumph for the navy, the war with France continued, and fear ran high that French forces might try to invade England.

The following year, on May 15, 1806, Betsy accepted a new role. She became an official visitor at the Quaker school and workhouse in Islington. The workhouse was a place where people who were unable to support themselves were offered basic accommodation and employment. England was dotted with workhouses, most of which were run by churches, with support from the government.

Although she was about to give birth to another baby, Betsy was determined to do a thorough job on her first visit to the school and workhouse. She took teacakes along with her for the workers and children and a Christian pamphlet to read to them. The children excitedly ate the teacakes and licked the crumbs from their fingers. They reminded Betsy of the "imps" she had taught to read in the laundry back at Earlham. After the children had eaten, they fell silent, and Betsy stood at the front and began reading aloud from the pamphlet, explaining its meaning as she went.

As she spoke, Betsy noticed that Ann Withers from the Gracechurch Street meetinghouse, who had accompanied her on the visit, began to sob quietly. It wasn't long before the teacher and then a number of the children began to weep as they listened. Betsy was stunned. Other than speaking at Quaker administrative meetings, this was the first time she had spoken openly to a large group about the love of Jesus and His gift of redemption and salvation. Even Betsy had to admit she was surprised by the words coming out of her mouth. Her words, steeped in her understanding of the poor and the issues they faced, seemed to deeply touch this group. They were wise words, yet Betsy felt that God was taking them and using them to touch the lives of those listening to her, even seasoned fellow Quakers like Ann Withers. The experience was as moving for Betsy as it was for the adults and children at the school and workhouse.

Two weeks after her first visit to the Quaker school and workhouse, Betsy gave birth to her fourth child, William. She and Joseph now had two daughters and two sons.

Following another bout of depression after the birth of William, Betsy continued her visiting schedule over the next two years and attended several family weddings. In December 1806 her sister Louisa married Samuel Hoare, a wealthy banker. Two weeks later her brother John married their cousin Elizabeth Gurney in a quiet ceremony. Marrying first cousins was frowned upon among the Quakers. Then five months later her sister Hannah made a much more popular match when she married Thomas Fowell Buxton, a long-time family friend and distant relative. After finishing his degree at Dublin

University, Fowell (he ordinarily used his second name) had turned down the opportunity to sit in the British House of Commons as the member from Dublin University. He didn't know what he was going to do next, but Betsy felt sure that he would make some kind of mark on the world.

In February 1808 Betsy gave birth to a fifth child, who was named Richenda after Betsy's sister. Betsy's sister-in-law, her brother John's wife, Elizabeth, was also pregnant, but tragedy struck when both she and the baby died in childbirth. Betsy raced to John's side at Earlham. She tried to comfort him, but he was overcome with grief and guilt at marrying his cousin, wondering whether that had caused his wife and baby to die. Betsy wondered if John would ever recover.

Another family wedding followed. This time it was Betsy's younger brother Sam, who married Elizabeth Sheppard from Ham House in Essex. At the same time the family's new Gurney Banking connections allowed Sam to get a position at Richardson and Overend, a prominent financial firm.

On August 20, 1808, Betsy contemplated her own future. She wrote in her journal,

> I have been married eight years yesterday; various trials of faith and patience have been permitted me; my course has been very different to what I had expected: instead of being, as I had hoped, a useful instrument to the Church Militant, here I am, a care-worn wife and mother, outwardly merely devoted to the things of this life.

Betsy was now twenty-eight years old. Her pattern of life looked settled, consisting of more pregnancies, more babies, and small acts of charity when she had the emotional and physical strength to make them happen. Neither she, nor anyone else for that matter, had any reason to suspect that her life was about to take a very different turn.

Chapter 7

A Bottle Long Corked Up

Betsy climbed the stairs to the guest room on the second floor where her father-in-law, William Storrs Fry, lay ill in bed. She entered the room and pulled the curtains open. Several goldfinches sat on the windowsill. "There, look at the birds. Thou canst see autumn's on its way," she said. "Imagine what it must be like at Plashet. Perhaps thou wilt be back there before the blackberries are picked and the chestnut tree is bare."

"Perhaps," William murmured as he stared out the window at the gray sky.

Although she now had five children, Betsy insisted that her father-in-law be brought to Mildred's Court when he became ill. She loved nursing the sick and was determined that he should have the best care. However, William's health did not return, and he died quietly in Betsy's home on October 15, 1808, at the age of seventy-two.

With the passing of her father-in-law, Betsy found her life had turned upside down. Joseph inherited Plashet, the Fry family's beautiful estate in East Ham, and he and Betsy and their children were expected to relocate there. Betsy was excited to be moving out of the dreary, smoky inner city of London to the countryside. She looked forward to taking peaceful walks in Epping Forest, feeding the fish in the ornamental ponds, and planting flowers in the formal gardens.

Betsy dreaded the thought of moving her household, however. It was a daunting task. The move had just gotten under way when she received an urgent message from her brother-in-law Fowell explaining that he and Betsy's sister Hannah were ill with scarlet fever. Fowell pleaded with Betsy to come and nurse them. He and Hannah were now living in London. Fowell had accepted a promising position with his uncle, Sampson Hanbury, who was part owner of a successful London business.

Although she would not have to travel far to nurse her sick sister and brother-in-law, Betsy hesitated. Scarlet fever was a deadly, contagious disease. Betsy wondered whether it was right to expose herself and therefore her children to it. But what else could she do? Her sister and brother-in-law needed her, and Betsy decided to go and assist them, trusting that God would keep her safe.

Thankfully, both Hannah and Fowell made a full recovery, and Betsy did not catch the disease. Better yet, Fowell had faced the thought of his own death and turned to God. He beamed as he told Betsy, "Whatever else happens, I am content to know that my Redeemer liveth." These words alone made the whole undertaking worthwhile for Betsy.

After nursing her sister and brother-in-law back to health, Betsy made a brief visit back to Earlham. She then returned to London and threw her energy into the moving process. By spring the Fry family was living in the large manor house at Plashet, with its parklike grounds. Betsy loved her new home. She took the children for long walks, pointing out the tadpoles in the pond and the bees buzzing around the apple blossoms. The walks reminded her of the happy times she'd spent as a child back at Earlham with her mother and sisters.

Betsy was expecting another baby, and she was glad it would be born in the country. The baby, Joseph Fry, named after his father, arrived on September 20, 1809. For once Betsy did not fall into a deep depression after the birth, although difficult news followed soon afterward. Betsy received a letter saying that Betsy's sister Priscilla at Earlham and her brother Daniel, who was in King's Lynn, had both contracted scarlet fever. Sarah Williman, the Gurney children's old nanny, had gone to King's Lynn to take care of Daniel. Another letter soon followed, saying that Sarah had come down with scarlet fever and died while caring for Daniel and that their father had undergone a serious operation but was expected to make a full recovery.

Then, when baby Joseph was just a month old, Betsy's sister Richenda arrived at Plashet by express coach to take Betsy back to Earlham. Their father had not recovered from his surgery. He was now gravely ill and was not expected to live more than a day or so. Betsy left her five older children at Plashet, bundled up the baby, and made a speedy trip north to Earlham, accompanied by her husband and Richenda. They arrived at Betsy's childhood home just after midnight on October 28, 1809. Betsy thrust the baby into Joseph's arms and rushed upstairs to her father's room. Her father was in a coma, but Betsy sat by his bed and stroked his hand.

At dawn John Gurney died. Since her mother's death seventeen years before, Betsy had dreaded losing her father too. She wept at his bedside and wondered how she would get through his burial at the Quaker burial ground on Chather Street in Norwich. Yet when the day of her father's entombment arrived, Betsy felt calm and peaceful. Her heart was still as Uncle Joseph spoke of her father's love and loyalty toward his sons and daughters. As Betsy stood surrounded by her sisters and brothers—Priscilla and Daniel still weak from their encounter with scarlet fever—she realized she had much to be grateful for and so many wonderful memories of her father.

A period of silence followed her uncle's speech, and Betsy found herself falling to her knees on the grass, not in grief but in thanksgiving. Without even thinking about what she was doing, she lifted her voice and declared, "Great and marvelous are Thy works, Lord God Almighty. Just and true are all Thy ways, Thou king of saints: be pleased to receive our thanksgiving."

When Betsy stood up, she realized everyone was staring at her, and she knew why. She had always been the shy one, the fearful one, the one who hung in the background, and here she was breaking the silence of her father's burial. She had become the thing she'd tried desperately to avoid—a religious enthusiast—and everyone knew it. Something deep inside Betsy had shifted. She felt liberated, alive. That night she confided in her journal, "I may be mistaken, but my own view of myself is this. I am a little like a bottle that has long been corked up and pressed down, and now there is an opening made, there appears much to run out."

Over the next few days, Betsy spent a lot of time talking to her brothers and sisters about her religious faith. She was shocked at how much had changed. Kitty, her oldest sister, had left the Quakers and been baptized into the Church of England, and Rachel and Richenda didn't seem far behind. Her younger brother Joseph John and younger sister Priscilla confided that they were leaning toward becoming Plain Quakers. Betsy was overjoyed and redoubled her efforts to pray for each of them.

When Betsy returned to Plashet, she was full of energy and looked around for something to do. Her attention soon rested on two problems. One was the elderly couple, a brother and sister, who lived in a large, dilapidated house just outside the gate to Plashet. Betsy had visited them several times and observed that their only income was from raising rabbits to sell. The money this brought in was not enough, and as a result the couple had no firewood gathered and no vegetables in the root cellar for the coming winter. Betsy had tried to talk to the couple about their needs, but they were too proud to accept any help.

The second problem Betsy focused on was the children around the estate. She noted that the laundress had three daughters who helped with the washing, and the coachman had a daughter who seemed bright and had taught herself to read a few words while she waited for her father behind the stable.

Betsy longed to set up a schoolhouse like the one she'd started at Earlham, with one exception—this time it would be a school for girls. The question was, where should she put the school? One day, while she was walking down a lane with her three oldest children, the answer came to her. Betsy would convince the elderly couple living just outside the gate to rent out rooms in their house for the school. That way they would have money to maintain their home and get through the winter, and the children could go to school. Betsy's mind raced. She knew the two people she needed to talk to next: the local Church of England vicar, Mr. Angelzark, and his wife.

Soon the meeting was organized. Vicar Angelzark and his wife were enthusiastic about the idea of a school and offered their full support. Next Betsy persuaded the old couple to rent out their living room to be used as the schoolhouse and asked an educated village girl, Harriet Howell, if she would be willing to teach the children. When Harriet agreed, Betsy paid for her to go to London and learn from her friend Joseph Lancaster.

Within three months of her father's death, Betsy had the school up and running. With the vicar's help, seventy girls were soon enrolled and had learned to read and write. Often they were the only ones in their family who could do so. Mostly the students owned no books, so when they passed a reading test, Betsy gave each girl a Bible.

With the school up and running, Betsy turned her attention to the health of the community. By now it was January and the ground was covered with snow. Betsy was concerned about how the babies and small children on the estate were faring in the freezing weather. As she had done at Earlham Hall, Betsy set aside a room in Plashet to cut and sew clothes. Soon she had piles of shirts, pinafores, and pants to distribute. Next she set up a soup kitchen in one of the barns. Anyone who was hungry could bring a bowl or pot and help himself or herself to the hot broth.

Once the soup kitchen was established, Betsy persuaded the family physician, Dr. Willan, to advise her on how to set up a dispensary that contained a mixture of bought drugs and local herbal mixtures. Betsy also firmly believed in the effectiveness of immunizations. She'd had each of her children vaccinated against smallpox, and not one of them had caught the disease. Now she decided it was time to inoculate every child in and around Plashet. She asked Dr. Willan to teach her how to administer the inoculation, and then she set to work. Soon Betsy had inoculated most of the children in the immediate area, after which she set her sights on Irish Row, about a half mile from Plashet.

Irish Row consisted of a line of cottages on either side of the road between Stratford and Ilford, where a number of Irish laborers and their families lived. These were the most rundown, ramshackle cottages Betsy had ever seen. The windows were covered with brown paper or were stuffed with rags in an attempt to keep out the cold. Pigs wallowed in the stagnant, polluted puddles in the muddy street, while scrawny chickens rummaged for scraps to eat. Women dressed in shreds of fabric moved about the street surrounded by groups of grubby, thin children.

Betsy set to work meeting the needs of the inhabitants of Irish Row. She handed out blankets and clothes, distributed food, administered medicine to sick children, discussed the importance of immunization, and encouraged children to attend school. The Roman Catholic priest overseeing the area welcomed Betsy and helped and encouraged her, even allowing her to distribute Bibles as gifts. Betsy was soon a regular visitor to Irish Row, where the inhabitants called her Madam Fry and would invite her to come and sit awhile in their cottages—even if the seat turned out to be no more than an upturned bucket.

With each visit to Irish Row, Betsy began to make headway in improving the lives of its inhabitants. She was delighted to see that the children were now better fed, healthier, and, along with their mothers, clad in warm, new clothes. A number of the children were learning to read.

During summer, bands of gypsies would camp in the lane near Plashet on their way to the Fairlop

Oak Fair in Epping Forest. Because the gypsies normally kept to themselves, Betsy was surprised when one morning a small, dark-haired boy knocked on her door. The butler alerted Betsy, who came to see what was the matter. The young boy explained in halting English that his sister was ill and that the family had heard there was a woman in the manor house who would help them. Betsy put some supplies into a basket and followed the boy back to the encampment.

At the encampment Betsy gave the sick child medicine and handed out clothes and Bibles. She then sat on the steps of the old gypsy caravans, many of them in disrepair (though not as much as the cottages on Irish Row), and talked to the parents and their children, most of whom were dirty and wore torn clothes. Sometimes she would pick up a small child and bounce him or her on her knee as she visited and talked about soap and water and the importance of vaccination. As she talked, the parents often went about their work, weaving baskets and the bottoms for chairs or sharpening scissors and knives on stone wheels while horses snorted from behind the caravans where they were tied up to graze. Soon Betsy was a regular visitor at the gypsy encampment.

The time passed quickly, and in February 1811 a daughter named Elizabeth, the Frys' seventh child, was born. She arrived a month early, tiny but perfect. The following month Betsy was accepted as a minister among the Quakers. This did not mean that she had any particular tasks but meant that she was endorsed by her meeting to teach and preach at other meetinghouses in much the same way William Savery and Deborah Darby had done.

On September 12, 1812, Betsy gave birth to another child, her eighth, and her fifth daughter, whom they named Hannah. The following month, the Fry family's business was in trouble, and the family faced the possibility of bankruptcy. Great Britain was still at war with France, with Napoleon and his army having marched all the way to Russia to try to capture that country. Part of Napoleon's strategy in fighting against Great Britain was to try to block European ports to British merchants. This, along with the fact that Great Britain was also involved in a war with the United States, had led to severe economic distress in England that resulted in a run on the banks, including Fry's Bank, in which large numbers of panicked customers withdrew their deposits. Things looked serious, and on October 18, 1812, it appeared that without help their bank would collapse.

In the face of this crisis, Betsy reached out to her family. On November 2, her brothers John and Sam and her cousin Hudson Gurney arrived in London and met at Mildred's Court to go over all of the Frys' financial holdings. After carefully analyzing the financial accounts of W. S. Fry & Sons, they came to the conclusion that the tea and spice business remained financially sound, while the bank was in peril.

The Gurneys agreed to loan the Frys money to keep their bank open, but the offer came with some strings attached. Some financial belt tightening was required. Because the enormous Plashet house was expensive to run, it would be closed up for the winter and the staff let go while Betsy and Joseph moved back to Mildred's Court to live. The four oldest Fry children, Katherine, Rachel, John, and William, would live with Betsy's uncle Joseph and aunt Jane in Norwich, who would feed and clothe them for a year. Betsy wept bitterly when she heard of these requirements, but she had little choice. The Gurneys would bail out the Frys financially, but only if they did as they were instructed.

Returning to London to live at Mildred's Court felt to Betsy like she had been sentenced to prison. Half her children had been taken away from her, and she had to leave behind the girls' school in East Ham under the care of Vicar and Mrs. Angelzark. Betsy stared out the window at Mildred's Court, where a drizzling rain had begun to fall on the gray cobblestones. Was this situation really God's will for her? Betsy didn't think so.

Chapter 8

Hell above Ground

It was February 1813, and from her window Betsy watched the snow fall onto the roof of Saint Mildred's Church and then slide off, landing on the ground. The street outside was almost deserted. *No wonder,* Betsy thought. *Who would venture out on such a cold day?* Then she spotted two men climbing out of a taxi carriage. The men were bundled up in overcoats and scarves, and Betsy watched as they paid the driver and trudged across the courtyard up to the door. Whoever they were, they were coming to visit the Fry home.

Minutes later Betsy was downstairs serving cake and hot tea to the men, who turned out to be Stephen Grellet and William Forster, two Quaker Friends she had recently come to know. Betsy was particularly impressed with Stephen. Seven years older than

Betsy, Stephen had been born into a wealthy family in France. His father was a counselor to King Louis XVI, and when the French Revolution broke out, Stephen had fought for the king. During the fighting he was captured and sentenced to be executed. He managed to escape and flee France, eventually finding his way to North America, where he heard Deborah Darby preach. Deborah had been visiting from England at the time, speaking in Quaker gatherings around the United States. Her preaching led Stephen to rethink his Catholic beliefs. After many conversations with Deborah, Stephen became a Quaker and then a traveling minister. Now Stephen and William sat warming themselves by the drawing-room fireplace.

Stephen spoke first. "My dear Friend Betsy, I am so grateful thou art home. I have a great need to unburden my soul of what I have seen," he said in French-accented English.

"What is it?" Betsy asked, wondering what could have shaken Stephen so much. As a traveling minister, Stephen had confronted some of the worst social situations in England, preaching in the style of John Wesley to huge crowds of thieves, pickpockets, and outcasts.

Stephen stood and paced the floor. "It was so bad I can hardly describe it to you. As you know, I have been visiting the prisoners at Newgate Prison, the *men* that is. Their situation is heart wrenching, particularly in this freezing weather. This morning William and I determined that we would see the condition of the women prisoners. The jailer tried to prevent us from going into the women's wing. He told us the women were unruly and desperate and if we entered, they would rip our clothes off and possibly kill us. He says he rarely goes in there himself, and never without the prison superintendent at his side. It took a lot of persuasion, but in the end he walked William and me to the women's wing of the prison and unlocked the door." Stephen stopped to sip his tea.

"How bad was it?" Betsy asked. From Mildred's Court she had often heard the prison bell toll and the crowd cheering in the distance, signifying that another prisoner had been publicly hanged on the gallows erected outside the jail. She also had heard Newgate Prison described as "hell above ground," but she did not know anyone who had seen inside the women's section.

Stephen shook his head. "I have never imagined anything so depraved," he said. "Many of the women were dressed in rags, their hair was matted, and lice crawled through it. They were black with filth and blood and knew no common human decency. They sleep in three tiers—one tier on the stone floor and two tiers of hammocks. When I first entered, the foulness of the air made me fall back. I saw two women fighting, trying to gouge each other's eyes out, and little babies, born right there and still naked. Some cried. Others appeared near death. Some of the women pleaded for help. Others scoffed at us and threw things at us."

"How terrible," Betsy said.

"But that wasn't the worst of it. The jailer took us upstairs to the sickroom. The women there were ill, some with the pox, lying on the bare floor or on old straw. One woman had just given birth. The room was very cold. The women had no one to nurse them and clean up after them and no medicines or bandages."

Betsy felt her heart lurch. Just over a mile from where she stood, women and children existed in conditions more deplorable than the slums she routinely visited. Why hadn't she investigated this before? Without a second thought she said, "Something must be done immediately for those poor, suffering children. I will go to them tomorrow. This afternoon I'll call in some Friends, and we'll make clothes for the babies."

The three of them talked for a few minutes, but Betsy was eager to get to work making clothes. By the next day she and a group of Quaker women had turned a bolt of green flannel into thirty baby gowns. Now Betsy faced the task of gaining permission to go inside the women's prison. Betsy had learned from Stephen that hardly any visitors were admitted.

Undaunted by the challenge, Betsy invited Anna, the sister of her brother-in-law Fowell, to accompany her to Newgate. The two women arrived at the large, windowless brick and stone building shortly before ten o'clock in the morning. Betsy had learned that Newgate actually housed three separate prisons. In the center was a large courtyard with cells opening onto it. This was the men's prison. To the left was a smaller courtyard and cells, which formed the debtor's prison, and to the right was the women's prison, which also consisted of a courtyard with cells opening onto it. At first Mr. Newman, the prison superintendent, refused to grant Betsy and Anna access, telling them that the inside of the jail was no place for women of their sensibilities. But Betsy stood her ground. After hearing a number of references to Betsy's family's wealth and influence, especially with various members of the government, the superintendent relented and pulled out a ring of keys.

Betsy and Anna were led down a long, dingy corridor lit occasionally by hissing gaslights. A pungent, gagging odor began to fill the air until Betsy felt sick to her stomach. The noise level rose from shrieks, shouts, and cries echoing along the corridor. Eventually the women came to a door made of iron bars. With no windows in the prison for ventilation, the odor was overwhelming. Betsy recognized the smells of alcohol, rotting food, human waste, and vomit. The noise from the other side of the door was deafening. The superintendent nodded at the surprised turnkey (warden), who unlocked the door with a flourish, swinging it open for Betsy and Anna to pass through. Betsy heard the door slam shut behind her and the key turn in the lock. In front of her and Anna was an iron grille through which Betsy had her first view of the inside of the women's wing of Newgate Prison.

What Betsy saw was worse than anything Stephen had described. In the dim light of the courtyard, the prisoners looked like ghosts. They were more wretched than any poor person Betsy had encountered in the slums of London or on Irish Row. Some of the women seemed crazed and animal-like, and others wept. The women clawed at the iron grille, begging for money to buy beer from their jailers, while trying to grab Betsy and Anna and drag them into the hell in which they existed. Betsy's heart beat rapidly as she asked the turnkey to unlock the grille and let her and Anna enter the courtyard. At first the turnkey resisted, telling Betsy that the women were animals who would attack and destroy her and Anna if he let them in. He said that he virtually never went inside, and if he had to, it was always with another turnkey.

Again Betsy stood her ground, pointing out that the women were not animals but human beings who deserved some human decency, which she intended to extend to them. Betsy and Anna had come with clothes for the babies, and they were going to distribute them. Besides, Betsy had committed herself into God's care, and He would watch over her and Anna. Reluctantly the turnkey opened the gate in the grille, and Betsy and Anna stepped inside. As soon as they were in the courtyard, the turnkey slammed the door shut behind them.

Silence fell over the courtyard as the women prisoners stared at Betsy and Anna. Then the women surged forward and surrounded them, some reaching out to touch them. Betsy forced herself to stand still as the women investigated her and Anna. She tried hard not to show any sign of shock or fear as she looked into the eyes of the women and saw nothing but emptiness and despair. She had never experienced anything like it in her life.

Betsy and Anna made their way upstairs to the infirmary and discovered it to be even more deplorable than Stephen had described. As Betsy and Anna began dressing the infirmary babies in the new flannel gowns the women had sewn, they cuddled the babies, trying to warm each one. The interior of the prison seemed even more frigid than it was outside. Betsy reached out and touched the mothers or held their hands in a gesture of love and friendship.

Over the next week, Betsy and Anna returned to Newgate Prison two more times, bringing with them children's clothes and fresh straw for the women to lie on. On her subsequent visits, Betsy learned that two classes of women prisoners were housed in the jail—transports and fines. The transports were those prisoners being housed at Newgate until there was room for them on the next ship taking prisoners to a penal colony in Australia. The fines were those who had been assigned short sentences for their alleged crimes. As Betsy soon learned, many of the fines had spent much more time in jail than they were sentenced to. This was because at the end of their jail term they had to pay a fee to the prison superintendent before they could be released. Since most of these women were desperately poor, they could not pay the fee and so were kept locked up in prison.

Before they left after their third visit to Newgate, Betsy and Anna knelt on the stone floor and began to pray. Much to Betsy's surprise, some of the women prisoners also knelt. Betsy felt so much pity for them that she began to cry, and the women joined in. Soon the prison yard was filled with the sound of weeping women. Betsy supposed they were weeping because of the fate that had befallen them and, by extension, their children. It was quite some time before Betsy got up off her knees, composed herself, and walked back down the long corridor and out into the fresh air.

Two months later, Betsy and her family returned to Plashet to live. Betsy was relieved to once again be out of the grimy city. The cherry tree outside the library window was in full bloom, and daffodils and yellow primroses dotted the lawns. Betsy was delighted when her four oldest children, Katherine, Rachel, John, and William, returned home from Norwich.

The girls' school Betsy had founded at East Ham was thriving under Mrs. Angelzark's leadership. Betsy would have liked to help the school financially, but money was short, and the Fry family was on a strict budget. Nor was Betsy able to do many of the other things she had previously done to help the poor in the local community. She had no money to provide medicine for the dispensary or for fabric to make clothes for the children. Betsy did manage to restart the soup kitchen, but gone was the hearty soup the kitchen used to serve, replaced by a watery broth that was cheaper to prepare.

The summer of 1813 passed quickly, with Betsy once again overseeing the day-to-day running of the large manor house and directing the servants. This, along with taking care of the children, kept her busy.

By September, Betsy knew she was pregnant once more, and she wrote in her diary, "I look upon it as one of the services of my life to bear children." However, she was worried about some of those children she had already borne. The oldest, twelve-year-old

Katherine and ten-year-old Rachel, had turned into argumentative, disobedient girls. They mocked Plain Quakers and told their mother they could not wait to get out from under her influence. Betsy was ashamed by their behavior, especially when she considered how her sister Louisa Hoare, a mother of six, was becoming an expert in early education and nursery discipline. Louisa was even writing a book on the subject, but none of the advice she gave Betsy seemed to work. Betsy could only hope and pray that her children would improve as they got older.

Betsy had other concerns, including how to provide for the new baby. Even though the Fry family was on a strict budget, Betsy found it almost impossible to stick to. The family always seemed to have more needs than money in the budget to meet them. Despite another bailout from Betsy's family, Fry's Bank continued to struggle. The only way to prevent people from withdrawing their money from the struggling bank was to make it look like everything was fine financially with the Fry family and their business. Betsy and Joseph tried hard to keep up appearances while they struggled to pay the bills for a household that included eight children, a governess, a tutor, eight indoor servants, and many outdoor ones. Betsy prayed they would make it through.

Betsy's ninth child, another girl, whom they named Louisa, was born in June 1814. Once again Betsy's sister Rachel had come to be at Betsy's side and help with the birth. While the two sisters were together, they agonized over their brother John. Since the death of his wife and baby in childbirth,

John had not been himself. In fact, sometimes Betsy feared that he would end up in an insane asylum (known today as psychiatric hospital). At times he did not leave his room for days, muttering to himself and refusing to eat. In September 1814, when baby Louisa was three months old, John died. It was a bitter blow for Betsy and her brothers and sisters. Her oldest brother, a man who had shown such promise, was dead at the age of thirty-three.

Following the death of her brother, Betsy struggled to remain focused on her family and her faith. She continued to try to influence her older children and teach the younger ones, but she was concerned about her namesake, four-year-old Elizabeth, called Betsy. The child was often sick with fever and wracked with pain. Betsy tried everything she could think of to help her daughter, but neither she nor the doctor could determine what was wrong. In November 1815, little Betsy died in her mother's arms. Her death was devastating for the entire Fry family. Betsy wrote about her daughter in her journal. "She had most tender affections, a good understanding for her years, a remarkably staid and solid mind. Her love very strong to her father and me, and her little attentions great; and remarkable in her kindness to servants, poor people, and animals."

The following year, 1816, was a grim year for the Fry family. In April Betsy gave birth to yet another child, a son whom they named Samuel Gurney Fry, though everyone called him Gurney from the start. By summer it was obvious that the Frys' financial woes were growing deeper. When Napoleon and his

French army were defeated in 1815, the war's end had made a dire economic impact on Great Britain. One in fourteen men had been engaged in waging the war, and scores of others had been involved in producing munitions and equipment for the fighting. These soldiers and workers were now returning home and looking for jobs—a strain on the British economy, and along with it, Fry's Bank.

Another meeting was called with the Gurneys to see what could be done about the situation. Betsy's brothers offered money to rescue the bank, though this time more stringent strings were attached. The Frys' household spending would be cut immediately: there was no more money for tutors or governesses, and the six oldest children would be educated elsewhere. Betsy was shocked as her brothers outlined their plan. Richenda and Joseph were sent to live with her brother Sam and his wife, Elizabeth, in Essex, where they would study with Sam and Elizabeth's children. John and William were sent to boarding school, and Katherine and Rachel would live with Betsy's sister Rachel and her brother Daniel at Runcton Hall in King's Lynn, where Daniel ran the local branch of the Gurney Bank.

Betsy found it hard to accept that she had lost control of her six oldest children. Her family would never be the same again, but she had no choice. The bank must be saved, and Betsy had to do whatever her brothers said to try to save it. She tried to concentrate on the three children left at home, four-year-old Hannah, two-year-old Louisa, and baby Gurney.

In November, Joseph, Betsy, and the three youngest children returned to live at Mildred's Court. This time Betsy was glad to be back in London and able to escape the empty, echoing rooms of Plashet. And now, with only three children to care for, she had more time on her hands. She was still a visiting minister among the Quakers, and she followed with interest the work of her two brothers-in-law, Thomas Fowell Buxton and Sam Hoare, who had joined together to found the Society for the Reformation of Prison Discipline. The organization, as its name implied, sought to bring about change in the penal code in Great Britain and in the way prisons were administered and run.

Over the years since her visits to Newgate Prison, Betsy had talked with her brothers-in-law about the deplorable conditions there. She had even accompanied Fowell and Sam on several visits. The conditions they had encountered convinced them that something had to be done. Both men were well connected—Fowell in particular knew a number of members of Parliament and ministers in the government—and they decided to use those connections to change British prisons.

Betsy loved to talk to Sam and Fowell about the prisons, and she admired their determination to improve conditions inside them. She knew that changes in the law were necessary to rectify the situation, but she also knew it would take a long time for that change to filter down to the people who needed it. Until then, the prisoners would continue to endure their hellish nightmare of being locked up.

Betsy recalled the days she and Anna had spent clothing babies in Newgate. She could not explain why, but those desperate women and children beckoned her back. On a bitter cold day in December, Betsy found herself standing once more outside Newgate Prison. Two things were different from her previous visits almost four years before. This time she had come alone, and she was not going to just provide clothing and then leave again. This time she would be persistent. Betsy felt confident that with God's help she could make the lives of the three hundred or so women and their children incarcerated there a whole lot more bearable.

Chapter 9

Opportunities for Good

Several days after Christmas 1816, Betsy stood beside Mr. Newman, the governor of Newgate, as he wrote a pass for her to enter the women's prison. "You will find some changes in there," Mr. Newman said, stamping the pass. "The women now occupy all six of the rooms allotted to them instead of just two, as it was when you were here before. The men no longer sleep in the other four rooms. The women have the whole yard and all the rooms to themselves. But I must caution you, Madam, that it is still an unfit place for a lady. I do not approve of you entering, but since you insist . . ." his voice trailed off as he handed over the piece of paper. Betsy knew that the governor had agreed to let her in only because of her family connections. He was clearly not happy being told what to do by a woman.

Minutes later Betsy was escorted down the dingy, gaslit stone hallway to the entrance of the women's prison. Once more the stench made her gag as she walked, and the noise level from inside the prison rose. As soon as the turnkey unlocked the barred door into the outer area of the jail, a hundred pairs of eyes rested on Betsy. Children cried, while some women wailed or jeered, and others poked wooden spoons tied to broomsticks between the bars, begging for food or money. Where previously there had been just a metal grille, there were now two rows of metal bars set a distance apart so that things could no longer be easily handed to the prisoners. To overcome this new obstacle, the women had improvised with wooden spoons and broom handles.

"This is as far as I'm willing to take you, ma'am," the turnkey said, stopping outside the barred door leading into the prison yard. "Permit or no permit, I ain't going to take responsibility for sending no lady into that there pack of wolves."

"Open the door, please," Betsy requested.

The turnkey shook his head. "Ain't no way I'm opening that door and letting you inside. No disrespect, ma'am, but they would eat you alive. I haven't got the manpower to drag you out when you get into trouble."

Betsy reached into her pocket and drew out twopence. She pressed it into the turnkey's hand. "This is for thy trouble, good sir," she said. "I will go in now, thank you."

The turnkey shrugged his shoulders. "If you insist," he said. "It's against all good judgment. That's all I'm going to say about that. Move aside, move aside!" With a rattle of keys, the turnkey opened the door.

Betsy took a deep breath and walked inside. The door clanged shut behind her. The women prisoners stood speechless for a few seconds. Even the babies stopped wailing. Then the women surged around Betsy, pulling at her clothes and reaching for her bonnet. Betsy looked around. She saw a young girl, about five years old, blonde like her own children. Immediately she thought of her daughter Betsy, who had died a year before. She still missed her deeply. Betsy reached out and lifted the girl into her arms. All was silent again.

Betsy looked from one woman to the next. "Friends, so many of you are mothers. I, too, am a mother. I am distressed for your children." The women started to murmur. *Perhaps they are waiting for a lecture,* Betsy thought. A wave of compassion washed over her as she went on. "Do you want your children to grow up to be criminals, to steal and curse and end up prisoners themselves? Is there not something *we* can do for these little ones?"

The women lowered their eyes and some began to cry. One woman pushed a chair toward Betsy and pointed for her to sit down. Betsy placed the girl on her lap and let her play with her gold watch chain. "Is there not something we can do for these little ones?" she said again.

Slowly, deliberately, mothers took their children by the hand and led them to Betsy. The children reached out to be hugged. Betsy pulled them close to her.

"I want better for my boy," one woman said, "but

I can hardly feed him. He were born in Newgate Prison. What hope is there for him?"

"My Joanie suffered from the cold awful like. She's had pus comin' out 'er ears, and now I don't think she hears unless I yell," another mother said.

One by one the mothers explained how impossible it was to look after their children in such a setting. Betsy completely agreed with them. She doubted she could do any better herself under the same circumstances.

It took several hours for the women to tell their stories, and when they had finished, Betsy pulled a New Testament from her pocket. "Now," she said, "I want to read you a story." She opened to Matthew, chapter twenty, and began to read aloud. "For the kingdom of heaven is like unto a man that is an householder, which went out early in the morning to hire labourers into his vineyard. And when he had agreed with the labourers for a penny a day, he sent them into his vineyard. And he went out about the third hour, and saw others standing idle in the marketplace, and said unto them; Go ye also into the vineyard, and whatsoever is right I will give you. And they went their way."

As Betsy read in her low, clear voice, the prison yard fell silent. The parable she read went on to tell how the master of the house had hired three more sets of workers at different times during the day and then paid them all the same amount at the end of the day. The ones who had been working the longest were angry that the master paid everyone the same amount. "God is like that," Betsy said. "It doesn't matter whether you have served and honored Him all of your life or if you turn from your sins now as a prisoner and try to serve Him here. It makes no difference. God accepts you, whoever and wherever you are."

"Really, Miss? That's not what we've heard from the chaplain. He makes a big point about our sins and all that, but he ain't got no talk of hope like you say, Miss, if ya know what I mean."

Betsy nodded. "That's why Jesus Christ came to earth, to forgive us our sins and make a pathway to God for each of us."

"This Jesus, who is He, Miss?" one woman asked. Betsy's eyes filled with tears. *If only these women knew the power and love of Christ, how different things could be in here,* she thought.

A week later Betsy returned to Newgate Prison, this time with an appointment to meet with Mr. Newman, the prison governor; the prison chaplain, Dr. Cotton; and two sheriffs from the City of London.

The intervening week had given Betsy time to ponder her conversation with the prisoners. The women had been astonished that she had asked them, "Is there not something *we* can do for these little ones?" They wanted to know if she really meant "we." Was she really asking them what *they* thought? And when Betsy told them that, yes, she did mean "we," tears welled in the eyes of many of the women.

The women explained that nobody had ever asked them what they thought about anything. In Newgate the turnkeys, who were all men, just bellowed at the women and told them what to do, as though they were animals. Many of the women confided that this was the first time anyone, inside or outside the prison, had ever wanted to know what they thought. Betsy understood this. Women in British society were not supposed to have opinions. Their role was simply to support men and do what those men decided was best. The women told Betsy what they wanted for their children—for them to learn so that they might have a chance at a different life for themselves.

As Betsy thought about this, she had come up with a plan—she would start a school for the children right inside Newgate Prison. She now had to convince the prison authorities to let her go ahead and do it.

One after the other Betsy looked the governor, the chaplain, and the two sheriffs in the eye as she laid out her plan for the school. The men sat stone-faced and silent as she spoke. When she was done, they dismissed the plan outright.

"Respectfully, Mrs. Fry," Mr. Newman, the prison governor, began, "I doubt you know much about schooling the poor. It is hard work."

Betsy wanted to jump in and interrupt the governor to tell him she knew quite a bit about educating poor children, but out of respect she stayed silent.

"But to educate the children of prisoners is impossible," Mr. Newman continued. "They are degenerate, like their parents, and quite unable to be taught. All they know is violence and disorder. These women and their children are the scum of the slums of London. Teaching them in jail is no role for a woman of London society. I simply cannot allow your plan to proceed," Mr. Newman concluded.

"Quite so," Dr. Cotton, the prison chaplain, chimed in. "These women and their children are debased and ignorant. They have no civilized life. They know no religious truth. All they know are those things that make them uncivilized—drinking, gambling, cursing, lasciviousness, and idleness—things that cannot be overcome in them, even by the noblest of women. I am afraid I must agree with Mr. Newman. This jail is no place for a school."

The two sheriffs nodded in agreement.

Betsy wasn't about to concede defeat. She believed that God had sent her to Newgate Prison for a purpose, and part of that purpose was educating the children. As politely as she could, Betsy assured the men she understood their reservations, but perhaps they might let her try the school for a short period as an experiment, since nothing like it had ever before been tried in a prison.

The men seemed to Betsy to be uncomfortable, even baffled, by her persistence and were not quite sure how to respond. Eventually the prison governor promised to look into the matter and meet with Betsy again in a week to discuss their decision, which would be final.

A week later Betsy met with the men. Mr. Newman informed Betsy that they had talked about her proposal. They wanted to support it, but there was just no available space in Newgate Prison to house a schoolroom.

"Space, then, is the only reason that thee will not allow the school?" Betsy asked.

After some hemming and hawing, the governor admitted it was.

Politely Betsy excused herself from the meeting, telling the men she would be back shortly. She headed straight to the women's prison yard, where she asked the women if they would make room for a school. The women agreed to make available one of the cells for the school, and they decided that Mary Conner, a woman from a respectable background who had been convicted of stealing a watch and sentenced to Newgate, should be the teacher.

Betsy headed back to the meeting. "I have good news for you, gentlemen," she announced. "I have just talked with the women inmates, and they have agreed to vacate one of the cells—giving themselves less room—so that there is room for a school for the children. Isn't that wonderful? Now there's no reason why we cannot move forward, is there?"

The men sat stunned. Mr. Newman was the first to speak. "I suppose, in that case, we must allow the school to go ahead," he said.

The following day, the first school ever set up inside a British prison began. Betsy, accompanied by her friend Mary Sanderson, arrived at Newgate with armfuls of old schoolbooks. Betsy gave Mary Conner instructions on how to use the books and teach the class. Then the students, thirty children in all, filed in. Most of them had been born in prison, though a few younger convicts also attended. Betsy would like to have been able to teach more of the children, especially the older ones, but no more than thirty could cram into the cell.

Through her involvement with the school, Betsy began to learn the various offenses for which the women had been convicted. As she listened to the crimes committed and the sentences passed out, she was shocked. The sentences were harsh compared to the crimes. The women pointed out to Betsy that she shouldn't be surprised. Up until two years ago, there were 222 crimes for which a person could be sentenced to death, and most of those crimes were trivial. Being in the company of gypsies for more than a month was a crime that carried a death sentence. (Betsy thought about all the time she had spent with the gypsies in East Ham when the family lived at Plashet. She wondered how close she'd come to being sentenced to death for doing so.) The malicious maiming of cattle, damaging Westminster Bridge, stealing from a shipwreck, writing a threatening letter, being a pickpocket—all were crimes that carried the death sentence, as did showing "strong evidence of malice" if you were a child between seven and fourteen. It was hard for Betsy to grasp that so many men, women, and children had lost their lives over the years for these petty offenses.

According to the women, things were a little better now. Magistrates no longer sentenced to death the offenders of some of the 222 crimes. Instead, in a display of compassion, they sentenced the offenders to be shipped to the penal colony in Australia, some for life, some for fourteen years, and others for seven years. As far as the women prisoners were concerned, it didn't matter whether it was seven years or fourteen years, it was still for life. After all, who could afford the cost of passage on a ship back to England from Australia at the end of her sentence? When the prisoners were led onto the ships for transport, they were as good as dead to England. Not only would they never see the land of their birth again, but also they would not be reunited with the families they had left behind.

Nearly sixty women were locked up in Newgate awaiting transport to Australia. The situation seemed so barbaric and so unfairly aimed at the poor. Rich offenders and those from upstanding families were given special treatment. They could afford to pay the governor to be housed in roomy cells away from the rest of the prison populace where they could bathe each day and enjoy palatable food. As far as Betsy was concerned, it might be called justice on the outside, but as she was discovering, it looked very different from the inside. And it spurred her on to teach the children and help the women in whatever way she could.

When Betsy tried to explain to her brother Joseph John what she was doing at Newgate, he was shocked. He pointed out that she was not mentally strong enough to handle such things. "If I don't, who will?" Betsy asked him. "I cannot leave it to a man. Men have abused the women in the prison so much that the women must be in charge and take care of each other." Joseph John had no answer for her.

Betsy was well aware that she was a lone woman in the world of men when it came to prison reform. It was rich and powerful men who were asked to be the patrons of new prison reform organizations springing up in Great Britain. But most of these men had never experienced the inside of a prison as she had. They were merely lending their names to what sounded like a noble cause. Betsy wished they could come with her, even for a day, into Newgate and see the things she had seen, touch the scabby, sick women and their children, smell the wretched stench that filled the air, and then watch thirty children learning to read and write in a cramped, dank, and decrepit cell off a noisy prison yard. Then they would know not only the challenge before them and their organizations but also the opportunities for good.

Betsy was attempting to do something women of English society did not do, and that reality sometimes overwhelmed her. She was haunted by questions. Was she up to the task? Would anyone listen to her? Support her? Encourage her? Yet she also felt that God had placed this opportunity before her. She was His hands and feet in Newgate. She was there to bring His comfort and hope to the women prisoners. She had to carry on.

Already a new plan was forming in Betsy's head. Since the opening of the school, many of the women prisoners had begged her to teach them not only how to read and write but also how to sew and learn other useful skills so that they could earn a living when they finally got out of prison.

With excitement Betsy told her reform-minded brothers-in-law, Sam and Fowell, that she was planning to train the Newgate women prisoners to do useful work. She expected them to be supportive and encouraging, but they were not. Didn't she know, they asked, that these women were the scum of the slums, and no amount of good intentions on Betsy's part would change them? They would steal the sewing equipment as well as the things that were made with it. A school in jail was one thing. Perhaps it would help a few bedraggled children. But didn't Betsy know that these women's natures were formed? They could not be reformed, even with all the care in the world. They were reprobates. They were too far gone to be helped. Surely Betsy could see that.

The truth was, Betsy couldn't see it. She stubbornly defended her plan. Her brothers-in-law were wrong, and she told them so. Yes, some of these women had made mistakes, committed crimes in the past, for which they were reaping the consequences. What they didn't need was more scorn heaped upon them. What these women in Newgate Prison needed was a chance. Was God too weak or too distant to care for them, to give them the chance they deserved? Betsy didn't think so.

While Betsy had hoped that Sam and Fowell and the Society for the Reformation of Prison Discipline they had formed would lend their support to her efforts in Newgate, she could see that that was not going to be the case. She decided to start her own support organization. In April 1817, four months after she had returned to Newgate Prison, the Association for the Improvement of the Female Prisoners in Newgate was formed. The group consisted of Betsy, ten other

Quaker women, and her old friend Mrs. Angelzark, the Anglican vicar's wife in East Ham, who ran the school Betsy had established near Plashet. Betsy had plans for change in Newgate Prison, and these women were behind her with their support. Let the men watch and learn what was possible.

Chapter 10

The Miracle at Newgate

Betsy stood in her parlor and read aloud. "The work of the Association for the Improvement of the Female Prisoners in Newgate exists to provide for the clothing, the instruction, and the employment of the women, to introduce them to the knowledge of the Holy Scriptures, and to form in them as much as possible those habits of order, sobriety and industry which may render them docile and peaceable whilst in prison and respectable when they leave it. Are we all agreed on that?" she asked.

The eleven other women in the room nodded. "Good," Betsy said. "With God's help, we will show what can be done. Based on what we discussed at our last meeting, I think it fair to say we all agreed that we will take turns visiting Newgate daily, that we will pay the salary of a resident matron, and that we will provide the funds necessary and arrange for the sale of handiwork." Again the women nodded. "And I have one more thing to say," Betsy continued. "I am happy to report that my husband is completely behind our work and has agreed to do whatever he can to bolster our cause." Betsy was grateful that although Joseph did not fully understand the passion that drove her to help others, he was willing to stand behind her and support her, unlike her brothers-in-law, Fowell and Sam, who both thought she had gone too far.

"In that vein," Betsy added, "next Sunday Mr. Newman, the prison governor, has agreed to attend a meeting of the women prisoners and me. I will put our plans to the women and ask if they are willing to abide by the rules and reap the rewards. I hope most of you will be able to attend."

The meeting continued with a discussion of the possible types of work the women prisoners could get paid for, and questions were asked about how to expand the Newgate school to include the prisoners as well as their children. When the first meeting of the association was over, Betsy felt it had gone well. Now she turned her attention and prayers to the upcoming meeting on Sunday. She knew her team needed to work *with* the prisoners and not just *for* them. If the prisoners were going to be helped, they would have to play a big part in the process. Betsy wrote a list of twelve rules of conduct that included the ways in which the matron and monitors would maintain discipline and orderliness in the prison and how the women could earn money doing piece-work knitting and sewing.

On Sunday Betsy met Mr. Newman in his office, and the two of them proceeded into the women's side of the prison together. Mr. Newman looked nervous. Betsy was calm. She believed the women would welcome the opportunity to create a better life for themselves, even if it was in prison.

Betsy was right. After she outlined the aims and proposed the rules of the Association for the Improvement of the Female Prisoners at Newgate, she asked the women to raise their hands if they agreed to the terms. Betsy watched as the women stared at her, some with open mouths. She knew most of them had never heard anything like this before, never been invited to give their opinion or to take part in their own destiny. Soon every hand in the room went up. Betsy turned to the governor, who, much to her surprise, had tears in his eyes.

Next Betsy told the women that the association already had their first contract. A women's clothing store in Fenchurch had agreed to buy knitted stockings from them. It was time to get to work. Before she left Newgate, Betsy read the parable of the barren fig tree, explaining to the women that although they had made mistakes, God was offering them a fresh chance to do things right.

Within a month, everything was working well. The women in the prison, dressed neatly in blue aprons, met at nine o'clock each morning to hear the Bible being read by one of the committee members and then broke into small groups, each supervised by a woman prisoner, to begin their day's work. As they knitted and sewed, their children were being taught in the next room. Visitors were astonished at how orderly and respectful the women were. Gone was the mass of half-dressed, half-mad women clawing at each other. Even Betsy could hardly believe the transformation. "I am ready to say," she wrote, "in the fullness of my head, 'surely it is the Lord's doing and marvelous in our eyes.'"

Just weeks later, Betsy and her committee were officially acknowledged by the City of London, who agreed to share the cost of the matron's wages. More and more visitors—royal princes, foreign dignitaries, and bishops—came to see what was being hailed as the "miracle" at Newgate, and each of them left impressed. Soon Betsy began receiving mail from all over England and the European continent. People, mostly women, wanted to know how they could start their own committees of women to work for the improvement of their local jails or how to start a prison school. Hundreds of magistrates wrote, asking about Betsy's methods and inviting her to visit them and help them set up similar programs in their prisons. So much mail arrived that Betsy could not open it all, much less read it and respond to it. She pressed her two oldest daughters, home for the holidays, into service, hoping that they would be inspired by all the sincere requests.

Although Betsy did everything she could to shy away from fame, it seemed that fame had found her. She was grateful for the support of her family. Joseph stood solidly behind her work, as did her cousin Hudson and Uncle Barclay, both of whom contributed large amounts of money to help buy clothes for the women. And Fowell and Sam, who had opposed her work at first, were now enthusiastic supporters. In fact, Fowell hoped to champion these causes as an elected official since he was running for office in the House of Commons and was promising prison reform.

The truth was, jails in Great Britain were bursting at the seams. There were about 107,000 prisoners, both men and women, and that number was growing steadily. As with the financial crisis in the country, this growth in incarceration was partly due to the end of the war against Napoleon's army. Over half a million soldiers and sailors had flooded back into Great Britain at the end of the war. The only thing these soldiers and sailors knew to do well was fight, and they had few other skills to help them to find jobs. At the same time, jobs were hard to come by, given the number of closed factories that formerly had made armaments for the war. As well, a revolution of mechanization was under way in Great Britain, with machines driven by steam engines doing the work of many men more quickly and efficiently, putting those men out of work.

With jobs so difficult to find, to keep themselves from starving, many unemployed men turned to crime, which in turn led to the swelling number of prisoners in Great Britain. Once in prison, these men (and the women already in prison) faced a grim future. Violent predators, petty thieves, and the mentally ill, both men *and* women, were more often than not all locked up in cells together. Those who were jailed for petty crimes, if they emerged as free men and women, often came out hardened criminals.

The deplorable conditions in the jails and the fast-growing prison population were forcing Parliament to confront the issue of prison reform, which Thomas Fowell Buxton hoped to promote if elected. He explained to Betsy that this was an urgent matter, since some members of Parliament believed prison life should be made harder, not easier, as a deterrent to others not to commit crime.

Not long after she began her work training the women prisoners at Newgate Prison, Betsy received an invitation to meet with the Lord Mayor of London. This was something Betsy had never imagined happening. Not only was she a woman, but also she had chosen to work with the poorest and most oppressed people in the city. Now the Lord Mayor wanted to meet with her and the women committee members of the Association for the Improvement of the Female Prisoners in Newgate. The Lord Mayor was cordial and seemed genuinely interested in the work among the women at Newgate, asking many probing questions, which Betsy answered as best she could.

At the same time that her fame was growing for her work among the women prisoners, Betsy came under close scrutiny from her fellow Quakers. At the yearly meeting of Quakers, members questioned Betsy's home life and her motives. They asked if she had deliberately sent away her six oldest children so that she could selfishly spend more time with the prisoners. Was she more interested in the prisoners' souls than those of her own children? And what about her husband—shouldn't he be the leader and she the follower in this endeavor? Betsy had few answers. Her six oldest children had been sent off to live with relatives by her brothers as part of the bargain to financially rescue Fry's Bank, and there was not much she could do about that. And while she was the one leading the work at the prison, her husband supported everything she did. Why was it so hard for others to grasp that women had leadership skills? Betsy prayed about this. She believed God had opened the door for her to be His hands and feet among the women prisoners of Newgate, and she asked Him to give her wisdom about what to do next as she visited the prison and oversaw the work of the association.

One matter that haunted Betsy was the public execution of four women prisoners she had worked with at Newgate. Although she had never witnessed an execution herself, from Mildred's Court Betsy had sometimes heard the prison bell and the commotion of the crowd when an execution was carried out. And in her time visiting Newgate, Betsy had learned all the sad details of a condemned prisoner's final hours—hours so cruel it was hard for Betsy to fathom that her fellow Britons and their leaders could have such callous attitudes toward another person's death. And now, in violation of justice and humanity, two women she knew, twenty-year-old Mary Ann James and thirty-three-year-old Charlotte Newman, sentenced to death for forgery, faced such a fate. Before their execution both women had written letters explaining how they had become Christians in jail and expressing their gratitude to Betsy and her committee members for teaching them about God and for extending their care and friendship. The two letters found their way into the newspapers, propelling Betsy to more fame and setting off a lively debate in England on the matter of public executions. Many people felt it was wrong for any human being to take another human's life. Others, who agreed with the death penalty, were still sickened that women who had committed petty crimes, in this case forgery, were executed along with murderers. While the debate continued, two more women prisoners Betsy had worked with at Newgate were executed.

All the publicity caused the upper classes of British society to become more aware of prison reform. On February 27, 1818, Betsy spoke to her most important audience yet, a parliamentary commission. As she rode to Parliament in the coach, with her brother Joseph John at her side, Betsy thought about how hard it had been years before for her to speak up for the first time in the yearly meeting of the Quakers. Then she had been among Friends. Now she was about to present her case for prison reform to the most powerful men in the nation. Adding to her nervousness was the fact that she would be the first woman in English history to address a parliamentary commission.

As she rode along, Betsy reached into her purse and pulled out a leather notebook into which she had written the three main points she wanted to cover. The first was religious instruction. Betsy had been surprised to learn that few of the prisoners at

Newgate had any knowledge of Christianity, Jesus, and the Bible. They were, however, eager to learn, and as they flocked to her Bible studies, their lives began to change. The Bible studies laid out a spiritual and moral basis on which the women could rebuild their lives. The second point had to do with categorizing the prisoners according to their crime and criminal history and then keeping the hardened criminals separate from those who had committed lesser crimes. And third, Betsy wanted to point out the importance of inmates producing something they could sell, first to support themselves while in prison and then to use that skill to earn a living once they were released. Betsy had a fourth point, but she was not sure whether she should dare to bring it up. It would all depend upon the mood of the men after she had talked about the first three points.

The meeting with the parliamentary commission started well. The men were respectful and interested in what Betsy had to say. When she had finished elaborating on her three points, one of the members asked if there was anything else.

"As a matter of fact, there is," Betsy replied. "The first three points are very important, but there is one other thing that must be done to ensure the safety of women in prison. I propose that we establish prisons especially for women and that these prisons employ women as wardens and inspectors, and that the only men who could be admitted would be a doctor or a minister of religion." Betsy stared at the astonished faces before her. She knew the men would be wondering whether women could even perform the tasks she proposed and, if so, where they were to be found. Women simply did not do that kind of work.

Betsy left the commission meeting satisfied that she had given the men much to think about. She prayed that Fowell would win a seat in Parliament in the upcoming August elections, knowing that he would help usher in the changes she had suggested.

Meanwhile Betsy had her hands full with another matter. She hoped to convince Home Secretary Lord Sidmouth to spare the life of Harriet Skelton. Harriet was another prisoner sentenced to death for passing a forged banknote, though she denied knowing the banknote was forged. Betsy had strong supporters, including Fowell's good friend William Wilberforce. Wilberforce was a member of the House of Commons, the lower chamber of Parliament in Great Britain, and Betsy was hopeful that using his name would sway Lord Sidmouth to spare Harriet's life.

Things did not go as Betsy had hoped. Lord Sidmouth told her that he felt the British public was getting out of hand in their calls for prison reform. The newspapers were filled with stories of unemployed weavers vandalizing the mechanical looms that had taken their jobs, and just the month before, the prince's carriage had been overrun by a mob of hungry people demanding bread. Although Lord Sidmouth felt sorry for Harriet, he was in favor of law and order. The alternative, he assured Betsy, would be a terrible revolution like the one that had occurred in France.

Betsy tried her best to change Lord Sidmouth's mind, and she enlisted everyone she could think of to help her, but it was no use. Harriet was executed on April 24, 1818. It was a bitter defeat for Betsy and her social reformer friends. Still, she did not give up. Another matter—the transport of female prisoners to far-off Australia—needed Betsy's immediate attention.

Chapter 11

Wretched Exiles

"You've never seen the likes of what's going to happen next, Miss," the turnkey told Betsy. "I don't care how well you think your women prisoners are—you wait till tonight."

Betsy grimaced. She had heard terrible stories about the night before the women prisoners were loaded onto carts and paraded through the streets of London to Deptford, where the ship that would carry them to Australia departed.

"Mayhem, Miss, that's the only word for it. The women—an' who can blame 'em—turn this place into a pigsty. They drink gin and curse at their fate, and then they attack anything they can get their hands on. They pull out each other's hair and break bones. Even the little 'uns aren't safe." The turnkey shook his head. "I've seen it all. But now, what with the knittin' needles and sewin' scissors in the workroom, I know they're all locked up and all, but I doubt that'll stop the women. It's a rampage."

"I'll have to do something about that," Betsy replied, grateful that Mr. Newman, the prison governor, had become one of her strongest supporters. She had an idea, but he would have to approve of it. An hour later Betsy was sitting in the governor's office.

"It is no wonder that the women riot in their cells," Betsy told Mr. Newman. "They are scared to death. Just think of it, they are about to go halfway around the world on a sailing ship. Most of them have never been more than a few miles from where they were born—many have never even seen the sea. What fate awaits them? None of us knows for sure. And to make matters worse, they are taken to the ship in open carts with jeering crowds lining the streets. I understand that people throw rotten vegetables and rocks at them. Can't we give them some dignity?"

"Dignity? For the prisoners? What do you have in mind?" the governor asked.

"Closed carriages," Betsy said. "If I can assure the women that they will be taken to the ship in closed carriages, I believe I can talk them out of drinking and fighting tonight."

Governor Newman raised his eyebrows. "I'm not sure that will be enough, but if anyone can convince them to behave, it is you. I am willing to give it a try."

That afternoon Betsy spoke to the women who were about to be transported to Australia. "It's a daunting prospect," she said, "but also an opportunity to trust in the Lord. You have heard that you will be at sea for up to five months, and the conditions will be rough. But I will go to the ship with you, and we will board it together. I will speak to the captain, to see what can be done for your comfort during the voyage and what plans he has for you once you land in Botany Bay. Once the ship sails, you will be outside the care of me and the committee, but God will be watching over you."

A murmur of approval came from the sixty women to be transported.

"Now, I have something to ask of you," Betsy continued. "I know in the past that lack of hope has driven women prisoners who are about to board the ship to extreme ends—drinking and violence—but I have spoken to Governor Newman, and he has agreed to convey you to the ship in dignity and safety. Your carriages will be covered, and no one will know you are inside. There will be no heckling or throwing of objects. In return, I ask that you remain calm and sober tonight. I will be praying for you, and I hope you will all do the same. I shall return in the morning to be with each of you."

The following morning, as Betsy entered Newgate Prison, the turnkey ran up to her and said excitedly, "Miss, I'd never 'ave believed it. The women were quiet as lambs last night. I even heard some of 'em singing like you taught 'em." He shook his head. "They call you the Angel of Newgate. You know that, don't you? Now I know why. Never thought I'd see the day."

Betsy smiled. She knew Mr. Newman would keep his word, and he did. Soon the sixty Newgate women prisoners, or transports, were lined up in an orderly fashion in the prison courtyard. They were chained together in groups of eight and then helped into taxi carriages. One by one the carriages made their way under the archway through the prison gate and out into the street. Betsy's carriage was the last to leave. Betsy sat solemnly with her Bible open on her lap and watched the procession of carriages in front of her as they began the five-mile journey to the dock at Deptford. The procession moved down Old Bailey toward Ludgate Hill and then across Blackfriars Bridge without drawing attention to itself. Betsy said a prayer of thanks as they moved along.

The sailing ship *Maria* sat moored at the dock. In addition to the sixty women from Newgate, another sixty women prisoners were assigned to the ship. Some of them had arrived via stagecoach, cart, or riverboat from all over England, Scotland, Wales, and Ireland. Many were still chained together or shackled at their wrists and ankles. Betsy's heart skipped a beat when she looked at the ragged bundle one woman carried and realized it was a baby. As cruel as it was to take a baby aboard ship, many of the women had left small children behind in poorhouses or sometimes with strangers. Other children arrived at the ship. Betsy was not sure why some mothers got to travel with their children while others did not, but she counted fourteen children on the ship's registry. Betsy knew she would have to do something about that situation in the future.

For now Betsy concentrated on the women in front of her. What did they need? What would they do aboard ship for so many long months? How could the women improve their lot while at sea? These were the kinds of questions Betsy loved to provide answers to. She talked with the ship's captain, Henry Williams, who gave Betsy permission to divide the prisoners into groups of twelve and assign each group a monitor, just as she had done in Newgate Prison. Betsy then called a meeting of the committee members of the Association for the Improvement of the Female Prisoners in Newgate. Soon the association arranged for fabric and yarn to be brought to the *Maria*, along with Bibles, prayer books, and other books that could be used to teach the women and children to read on the long voyage ahead.

On Friday, May 15, 1818, the *Maria* prepared to set sail for Australia. Captain Williams ordered all of the women and children to line up on the quarterdeck so that Betsy could address them one last time. Betsy opened her Bible and looked across the crowd of faces. Sailors nearby were climbing the ship's rigging to take in the unusual sight as Betsy began reading the story of the prodigal son. A hush fell over the group on the quarterdeck, and soon even the sailors on the nearby vessels took off their hats and stopped yelling. Only the cries of seagulls and the lapping of water against the side of the ship broke the silence. When she had finished reading, Betsy knelt on the deck and prayed for the captain, the crew, and the convicts being transported on the ship, commending them all into God's care.

Betsy then bid the women farewell, and Captain Williams escorted her off the vessel. Betsy stood on the dock and watched as the *Maria* was pulled into the current of the Thames River. She heard the captain give the order to hoist the sails. The sails billowed in the breeze, and the *Maria* departed. Betsy stood and watched until the ship disappeared from view around a bend. It was the start of a fifteen-thousand-mile voyage that would take the convicts down the Thames, past Gravesend, and out into the North Sea. Within hours, the women would catch the last glimpse of their homeland, a sight Betsy knew most would probably never see again.

The following Friday Betsy was back at Newgate Prison, conducting her usual Friday-morning Bible study. Following the publication of the report she had delivered to the parliamentary commission, Betsy had become even better known across Great Britain. Even Queen Charlotte had stopped to talk with her when the two women crossed paths at the Mansion House in London several weeks earlier. Betsy was as astonished and delighted as the other women in attendance. It was almost unheard of for the Queen of England to stop and address a commoner such as Betsy.

All this fame and attention concerned Betsy. As unbelievable as she found it, some wealthy people came to the prison Bible study in the chapel because it was the fashionable thing to do. Betsy wondered if she should even continue speaking at the meetings, since she attracted so much attention. In the end she decided the matter was in God's hands.

Betsy realized that she had become a voice for the voiceless—the prisoners in Newgate Prison.

Not only that, but she continued to get a steady stream of letters from across the British Isles, both from prisoners and from people wanting to set up committees to help prisoners. Betsy decided to take action. In August she set out with her fifteen-year-old daughter, Rachel, her brother Joseph John Gurney, and his wife, Mary. Together the Fry and Gurney group planned to speak at Quaker meetings. Betsy and Joseph John were now both certified to preach at Quaker events and public meetings and to visit and inspect prisons in northern England and Scotland.

Shortly before Betsy set out on the trip, her brother-in-law Thomas Fowell Buxton was elected to the British Parliament to represent the district of Weymouth. Now that he was elected, he was in a position to promote Betsy's work in particular and prison reform in general in the House of Commons.

Leaving the rest of her children with her husband, Joseph, at Plashet, where the Fry family was once again living, Betsy and her brother and their entourage set out on the journey from Earlham in a convoy of carriages accompanied by footmen and servants from the manor. As the group traveled, local newspapers reported on Betsy's activities. Large numbers of people showed up to hear Betsy and her brother speak at both Quaker and general meetings. Betsy would talk about the challenge of prison reform in Great Britain, her experiences in Newgate Prison, and how the programs she had established there were having a deep impact on the lives of the women prisoners and their children.

She also challenged the women who attended the meetings to band together into local committees, much like the association Betsy had established in London, and begin to work with the prisoners in their local jails.

Betsy and Joseph John visited as many prisons as they could. Some of the prisons were reluctant to allow this, but because of all the attention Betsy was receiving in the newspapers, local prison governors let her and Joseph John inside. They even gave them permission to mingle with the prisoners and talk to the turnkeys. The officials were amazed at the respect with which the prisoners regarded Betsy.

In almost every jail, Betsy found deplorable conditions. Many times men and women prisoners were locked up together in damp, dingy, overcrowded cells. The floors were covered with moldered straw for them to sleep on, and a single wooden trough served as a communal toilet. The prisoners had nothing to occupy their time during the day. Instead they would sit and drink, since an ample supply of alcohol seemed to find its way into every prison Betsy and Joseph John visited. When intoxicated, the prisoners fought among themselves and created all kinds of mayhem.

One of the things that greatly concerned Betsy was the way mentally ill prisoners were treated. These prisoners were either chained up and locked in dark cells or allowed to mingle with the general prison population where they were mocked and taunted and sometimes beaten up. Betsy had great compassion for these prisoners. Suffering from depression as she did, she knew how easy it was to slip into dark, irrational places in the mind. She was particularly touched by a mentally ill man she encountered in the jail at Haddington, near Edinburgh, Scotland. No one knew where the man had come from when he was arrested for damaging a garden seat at the home of a local nobleman. For eighteen months he had been chained up and kept in solitary confinement in a cold, dark cell.

In Glasgow, Scotland, the governor of the local prison was resistant to Betsy's visiting the women prisoners. He told her that it was dangerous to go among them, that they didn't like to read or listen, and that all they were interested in was ridiculing the turnkeys and trying to attack and kill them when they had to enter the cells. Still, Betsy prevailed, and the governor allowed her to visit the women. Surrounded by the women prisoners, Betsy stepped into the courtyard, took off her bonnet, sat down on a chair, and silently looked into each woman's eyes. Instead of attacking her, as the governor had predicted, the women sat and waited for Betsy to speak.

"I had better tell you what we have come about," Betsy began as she went on to tell them what she had done in Newgate Prison in London and how it was changing the women prisoners' lives. The prisoners sat in rapt attention as Betsy spoke. "Would you like it if ladies would visit you and speak comfort to you and help you to be better?" she asked. With that, Betsy read aloud the rules that governed the program at Newgate and asked the women to raise their hand if they agreed with the rules. At first no one put up a hand. Betsy sat silently looking at the prisoners, and then she began to hear sniffles and sobs. She then noticed tears cascading down some of the women's cheeks. Soon every woman prisoner had her hand raised. Betsy took out her New Testament and read two parables, one about the lost sheep and the other about the prodigal son. Before leaving the jail, she knelt on the courtyard and prayed for the women prisoners.

Betsy smiled at the prison governor. She knew he was stunned by the outcome. He had expected the women to riot and attack Betsy. Instead the prisoners had sat meekly before her and signified they would like women to come and work with them in the same way she worked with the prisoners at Newgate. Betsy knew that the stunned governor would not stand in their way.

By the time she returned to Plashet after her two-month trip, Betsy was exhausted, unusually so. She soon realized that at age thirty-eight she was once again pregnant, this time with her eleventh child. However, the pregnancy did not go well, and Betsy went to Sussex and Kent to rest. During the difficult following months, she tried to stay focused on her mission. She culled through the notes on her recent trip north and, with Joseph John, wrote a report titled "Prisons in Scotland and the North of England," which was published in 1819.

Other matters weighed on Betsy. It seemed as if the poor and needy from all over the world were reaching out to her. A missionary visiting from India told Betsy of the practice of sati, a custom in parts of

India where a widow burned herself to death, either on the funeral pyre of her dead husband or in some other way soon after his funeral. Betsy was shocked as the missionary explained to her that in the province in which she worked in India about seven hundred widows per year burned themselves to death. Betsy decided to do something about the situation. She talked the matter over with Fowell, who agreed to mount a campaign in Parliament to have the practice of sati banned in all of British India.

In February 1819 Betsy received a letter from Australia. She opened it and began to read.

> Having learned from the public papers, as well as from my friends in England, the lively interest you have taken in promoting the temporal and eternal welfare of those unhappy females who fall under the sentence of the law, I am induced to address a few lines to you respecting such as visit our distant shore. It may be gratifying to you, madam, to hear that I meet with those wretched exiles who have shared your attention, and who mention your maternal care with gratitude and affection.

The letter was from Samuel Marsden, the highest-ranking Church of England clergyman in New South Wales, Australia. Marsden's letter went on to explain that when the women convicts arrived on ships from England, there was no proper place to accommodate or feed them. To survive, many of the women convicts turned to crime to eke out a pittance on which to live. "All the female convicts have not run to the same lengths in vice," Marsden noted. "All are not equally hardened in crime. And it is most dreadful that all should alike, on their arrival here, be liable and exposed to the same dangerous temptations, without any remedy." Marsden also noted that for twenty years he had been seeking a remedy from Great Britain, pleading with political and church leaders, asking that they provide a proper barracks in which to house the women prisoners they were sending by the shipload to Botany Bay.

On reading Marsden's letter, Betsy took up his cause. She and the members of her committee began to press the case with political leaders and the rich and powerful of London society that something needed to be done about the women prisoners' situation.

In May 1819, the stillbirth of Betsy's baby plunged her into another deep depression. The committee took over her portion of the prison work while Betsy sat throughout the summer staring blankly out the window, her mind riddled with dark thoughts.

In the fall, Betsy rallied from her depression. It was time for her to get back to work. This time it was the homeless in London who needed her.

Chapter 12

New Challenges

Betsy rubbed the window of her carriage. It was only three in the afternoon, and already ice was settling around the edges of the window, making it difficult for Betsy to see out. She peered at the bleak, white scene. A bitter winter had settled over the British Isles. Snow lined the streets of London and was piled high on the roofs of buildings and houses. Long icicles clung to the edges of the buildings while men and women in the street wrapped themselves in thick coats. As she peered out the window, Betsy frowned. What was that on the step of a cloth merchant's shop? A bundle of rags, she thought, or perhaps . . . "Stop the carriage," she called out while tapping her hand on the roof.

The horses came to a halt, and the footman opened the door. "What is it, ma'am?" he asked.

"I need to get out," Betsy replied. "Come walk with me."

The snow crunched beneath Betsy's feet as she climbed out and walked toward the bundle of rags, with the footman beside her. Soon her eyes clouded with tears. As she had suspected, the bundle of rags was attached to a body—that of a small boy about five years old. As Betsy approached, she could see that the boy's skin was blue and his eyes were rolled back in his head.

"He's gone, ma'am," the footman said. "Just too cold out 'ere for a little 'un."

Betsy nodded as she bent down to feel for a pulse. There was none. "Thou art right," she said, looking around. "I wonder who the lad belongs to."

"Could be anyone," the footman replied. "The likes of those who let their sons dress in tatters on a freezing day don't have no money for a funeral. He won't be claimed."

"I suppose not," Betsy said, looking up and down the street. A few people peered around the edges of buildings, intrigued with why a fine carriage had stopped in such an unusual place. Betsy studied their clothes of thin cotton fabric. Some had holes in their shoes and wore no socks. "Likely more will die," Betsy said. "This is a cruel winter. They must get indoors. That's where this lad should have been."

"Easier said than done," the footman noted.

"True enough," Betsy said. "I'll walk the rest of the way home if thou wilt take the body to the morgue and see that he gets a pauper's burial."

For the remainder of the walk home to Mildred's Court, where the Fry family was again living for the winter, Betsy silently studied those she saw along the way. Some were well dressed with hats and gloves and woolen coats, but others wore flimsy cotton clothes. *Many more will die,* she told herself, *unless they get inside on these freezing nights.*

By the time she arrived home, Betsy had a plan. "Think of it," she told her husband, "little children freezing to death outside our own doors. Something must be done!"

Joseph nodded in agreement. "What do you have in mind?" he asked.

Betsy smiled. This was what she loved about her husband, who was always willing to support her ideas. "I was thinking that Sam and Fowell and some of their friends could help. I shall send a servant to ask for them right away."

Within an hour an unofficial committee was sipping tea in Betsy's parlor. Betsy told her two brothers-in-law what she had seen. "We must set up somewhere warm for the houseless to shelter at night," she said. "If we don't, many will freeze to death, especially the children."

Everyone agreed, and Sam offered to ask his friend Oliver Hick of Cheapside if he had a warehouse that could be used for the purpose. Later that night, news came that Oliver was willing to provide a warehouse for a shelter in London Wall. The following morning Betsy rallied the members of the Association for the Improvement of the Female Prisoners in Newgate to collect donations. When combined with donations from Sam and Fowell, the collection provided enough to buy straw, soup, and bread. Within twenty-four hours of Betsy's seeing the dead boy on the step of the draper's shop, the first nightly shelter for the "houseless" was opened in London. Betsy and her Quaker friends worked tirelessly to provide food and shelter for the city's poorest residents.

As she worked, Betsy realized that many of the men were unemployed, and she used her connections with the Merchant Seaman's Society to try to find them jobs.

Over the next few months, about two hundred people a night sought shelter in the warehouse. On particularly cold nights, up to eight hundred people would be crammed into the building, grateful for a place to be out of the bitter cold.

Rallying her friends and contacts to help the homeless gave Betsy a renewed sense of purpose. Betsy resumed regular involvement at Newgate Prison, where committee members had been doing a fine job in her absence. She also continued to visit convict ships carrying women prisoners bound for Australia. Each voyage was a little better organized than the previous one. Before long the Association for the Improvement of the Female Prisoners in Newgate was equipping departing women with large burlap bags containing aprons, a bonnet, a measuring tape, a hundred sewing needles, and an ounce of pins—items needed for them to do useful work upon their arrival in Australia. On each of the ships, the committee also installed libraries stocked with religious books and biographies and with books containing stories of travel and adventure. Not only could the books be used to teach women to read on the voyage, but also those who could read would have something with which to engage their minds during the long trip south.

Bags filled with mail continued to arrive for Betsy. One letter in particular caught her attention. It was from John Venning, an Englishman living in Saint Petersburg, Russia, who wrote to tell Betsy he had been so inspired by her stand against injustice for criminals and the mentally ill that he was conducting his own survey of prisons and asylums in Russia. Furthermore, he intended to present his findings to the Russian emperor and his wife. Betsy could only thank God that her example of kindness was being followed in a faraway place.

Closer to home Betsy had new concerns. Fowell and Hannah Buxton's oldest son returned home from boarding school with inflammation of the lungs. He was gravely ill, and Betsy rushed to his side to nurse him. Sadly, he died just as his younger sister contracted whooping cough and measles. Within a month, three of the boy's little sisters had also died. All four Buxton children were buried in a single grave. The marker on the gravestone simply read *Ehue*, the Latin word for "Alas." The Buxton family had gone from six children to two. Heartbroken, Hannah and Fowell sold their house and moved to Cromer Hall on the Norfolk coast of England. A month after the deaths of her three nieces and nephew, Betsy turned forty years old. In her grief, she did not feel like celebrating.

Betsy's favorite sister, Priscilla, had begun spitting up blood. This was not a good sign, and Betsy soon realized that her thirty-five-year-old sister had tuberculosis. A year later, Priscilla died. Now there were only six Gurney sisters alive. The chain had been broken.

Even in her grief, Betsy continued the work she felt God had called her to do. When more letters arrived from around the British Isles asking for advice on prison reform, she founded the British Society for Promoting Reformation of Female Prisoners. The Duchess of Gloucester became the society's first patron. Betsy's reach had extended far beyond London.

Family matters continued to trouble Betsy. Her second oldest daughter, Rachel, had been particularly willful and moody for several years. Now, to Betsy's shock, she learned why. Eighteen-year-old Rachel had been secretly courting Frank Cresswell for the past four years. Frank was a captain in the British army and had just returned from service in India. He and Rachel had fallen in love sometime before he departed for India. It was astonishing news and a disappointment to Betsy, who had hoped that Rachel would marry a Quaker.

The extended family met together under the leadership of Betsy's cousin, Hudson Gurney, to decide what should be done about the situation. Betsy remembered how, years before, her sister Rachel had fallen in love with Henry Enfield, a non-Quaker. The family had told Rachel to break off all ties with Henry, and as a result she had never married. Now her namesake Rachel awaited her fate. This time, the family was more understanding. Times had changed, the younger ones argued, and

Rachel should be allowed to marry for love. Betsy was not so sure. If Rachel married outside the Quakers, Betsy's Plain Quaker friends would insist that she and Joseph not attend the wedding or encourage the marriage in any way.

Hudson ultimately announced that Rachel and Frank could marry. Betsy braced herself for a volley of criticism. It was every bit as hurtful as Betsy thought it would be. So was the thought of not attending her daughter's wedding. But if she wanted to remain a Plain Quaker, Betsy had no choice but not to go.

On August 23, 1821, without her parents or older sister, Katherine, present, Rachel Fry married Captain Frank Cresswell. Betsy recorded her thoughts in her diary: "My dearest Rachel married at 9 o'clock. I deeply felt about that time a sweet feeling was my portion though certainly very low. Visited the widows, the fatherless, my poor Kate with me. Quietly at home the rest of the day." Betsy soon found that Rachel was much happier as a married woman than as a lovesick teenager.

In the fall, Betsy and Joseph, accompanied by their daughters Rachel and Katherine, toured northern England. They visited prisons in Nottingham, Lincoln, Wakefield, Sheffield, Leeds, York, Durham, Newcastle, Carlisle, Lancaster, and Liverpool, establishing women's committees to work with women prisoners along the way.

The following spring, Betsy realized that she was expecting another baby. Much to her surprise, when she told Rachel, her daughter confided that she also was pregnant. Both women gave birth to sons on the same day, November 1, 1822. Betsy named her son Daniel Henry Fry, and Rachel named hers Frances Joseph Cresswell. In a single day Betsy became both a mother for the twelfth time and a grandmother for the first time.

Betsy quickly rebounded from the birth of another child and continued her work. The opportunities to encourage change within the British justice system continued to increase. In March 1823 Betsy and Joseph, accompanied by Fowell, met with the new home secretary, Robert Peel. Betsy was impressed with the new home secretary, who was younger than his predecessor, Lord Sidmouth, and had very different ideas. While not a natural reformer, Peel explained that if Great Britain was to be a powerful nation at home and abroad, things at home needed to be administered in a more centralized way. This included Britain's social policy, under which fell prisons and the country's antiquated legal system. Peel believed these things could no longer be left to local authorities to administer. The government in London needed to take a stronger hand.

The meeting with Robert Peel energized Betsy. Now, like never before, it appeared to her that key players—including Peel, William Wilberforce, and her own brother-in-law Fowell—were lining up to reform the criminal and poor laws of the British Isles. It was not a time to sit idly by, and Betsy tried to make the most of every minute. She spoke loudly and clearly on reform issues and the abolition of slavery. Joseph, though, was not as enthusiastic about his wife's extra workload. He told Betsy he had imagined the two of them slowing down now that they were grandparents. To help Betsy understand how serious he was about this, he bought a tract of land near Dagenham, situated in the marshlands along the Thames. The property consisted of two small cottages surrounded by willow trees and was accessible only from a rough cart road through the marshes or by boat from the river. Joseph would take the children to the property on weekends to relax and fish. At first Betsy was reluctant to go to the new property, especially since fishing was a frivolity Plain Quakers frowned upon. But she soon began to join the family and found the time spent there to be soothing and relaxing, far away from the pressure for social reform. She even stopped fretting over the fact that Joseph found fishing such an enjoyable pastime.

In 1823 Betsy's faith in Robert Peel was rewarded when the Prisons Act, which he had crafted, was passed into law by Parliament. The act contained many of the things Betsy had been pushing for. Turnkeys and prison guards were to become salaried employees and were no longer allowed to collect fees from prisoners to secure their release at the end of serving their prison sentence. Prisoners were to be properly classified so that hardened criminals were locked up together and would be unable to influence those serving petty-crime sentences. In prisons that housed both men and women, the sexes were to be separated and the women watched over by female wardens. The use of irons and solitary confinement was abolished, and standards were laid out for the health, clothing, food, education, and work of prisoners. The prisons were to seek to reform prisoners rather than punish them, and justices of the peace were empowered to investigate the complaints of prisoners if they thought their sentences too harsh.

It was all wonderful to Betsy, except for one thing. In many parts of the British Isles, the new law was resisted by local officials who still clung to old ideas. This resistance was disappointing for Betsy, who had hoped that the requirements of the Prisons Act would be eagerly embraced, and she continued to push for full adoption of all the requirements.

During this time Betsy continued to be torn between taking part in the politics that surrounded reform and the desire to be a good Plain Quaker and stay out of worldly matters. The desire to see real change in the country almost always won out, and this time was no different. Betsy kept busy touring the country, inspecting prisons, and rallying people to rise up and bring about change.

All of these efforts took their toll physically, and by summer 1824, forty-four-year-old Elizabeth Fry needed a complete change of scenery. Rachel offered to look after the younger children while Joseph and Katherine, the eldest Fry daughter, took Betsy to stay at the seaside in Brighton. At first Betsy spent most of her time lying in bed or sitting at the window staring out to sea. Sometimes she was aware of someone knocking at the door and muted conversations taking place in the parlor. Betsy knew that word had leaked out that she was staying in Brighton. Many people arrived at the door, hoping to meet her, but she was too weak to talk to anyone, and Joseph and Katherine sent them away.

Betsy had trouble sleeping through the night and often sat and stared out into the darkness. She began to notice that a lone man walked the beach every three hours, night and day. It did not matter whether the weather was sunny or a terrible storm was brewing. A man, sometimes a tall one with blond hair, sometimes a shorter one with an uneven gait, trudged down the shingle beach, turned at a large rock on the foreshore, and trudged back again. Betsy wondered what they were doing. Joseph informed her they were blockade men, whose job was to prevent smugglers from landing along the coast.

As she continued to watch the men night after night, Betsy felt sorry for them. They looked so lonely. One day, while she was out in her carriage, she passed the blockade station. Betsy had the driver stop, and she went inside to investigate. As she opened the door to the blockade station, three small children were staring at her. A young woman, whom Betsy presumed to be their mother, rushed into the room and ushered the children out.

"You can't be in 'ere, ma'am."

Betsy turned to see the shorter man who patrolled the beach walk through a door to her left. "Why ever not?" she asked.

"Blockade men aren't supposed to talk to regular folk. It's forbidden. We've got our job to do, we 'ave, and that don't include being friendly with folk."

"Well," Betsy replied. "My name is Elizabeth Fry. I was looking forward to hearing about thy job, but since thou canst not talk to me, please give this to thy superior officer." She reached into her purse and handed the blockade man her calling card.

"I can do that, ma'am," he said.

Two days later Betsy heard a knock at the door of the cottage where she was staying in Brighton. A naval lieutenant, the commander of the blockade station, had come to visit her. Betsy welcomed the man into the parlor.

"Pleased to meet you, madam," the commander said, taking off his hat. "I've heard so much about you, and now here I am meeting you in person. Was there some reason you came to my station? Something I can help you with?"

Betsy nodded. "Couldst thou explain to me how the blockade men work? I have seen them walking the beach, but I didn't realize they are forbidden to talk to anyone."

"It's for their own good, ma'am," the commander said as he sipped a cup of scalding tea. "The blockade men serve a useful purpose. They guard against smuggling, marching the coast at regular intervals, always on the outlook for illegal activity. Because of this they are not well liked by the smugglers or by the locals who consume the smuggled goods. They are forbidden to talk with people lest they get into arguments or are offered bribes by smugglers and locals to not interfere with the smuggling.

"I see," Betsy said. "But aren't they lonely? What do the men do when they're not on patrol? And how about their sons and daughters—do they attend school?"

"Not often," the commander replied. "Most of the blockade stations are located in remote places, far away from any school, and the men can't afford boarding school on their pay."

"Oh dear," Betsy said, her mind whirling. She thought about how the Association for the Improvement of the Female Prisoners in Newgate was now stocking every convict ship leaving England with a library of books for the convicts to read on the long voyage to Australia. She wondered if the blockade stations could benefit from something similar. "Do the children have books, or even the blockade men themselves?" she asked.

The commander shook his head. "Not many of them, ma'am. Though the men are required to read, most of their children cannot. Books aren't cheap, as I'm sure you know."

"Quite so," Betsy said, "but I believe they would be greatly appreciated, doesn't thee?"

"I am sure they would," the man replied.

"Well, then, commander, let me see what I can do to start libraries for thee and thy men. On the convict ships we provide books with religious themes, as well as travel and adventure books and good biographies."

"That would be most appreciated," the commander said.

"How many blockade stations are there along the coast of Great Britain?"

"There are several hundred such stations encompassing the coast of the British Isles, manned by over thirty-five hundred blockade men and their families," the commander informed Betsy.

Betsy had been at Brighton for three months, long enough for her to watch the leaves on the oak trees turn to autumn colors. She left stronger now—partly because of the rest and partly because she had a new project on which to focus. It was time to return to London and set about establishing libraries for the blockade men and their families. Nothing energized Betsy more than the thought of helping someone else. Little did she know she would soon be the one in need of help.

Chapter 13

The Disaster Lurking in the Shadows

On a cold day in November 1825, Betsy visited the school she had founded over fifteen years before at East Ham, just outside the gates to Plashet. The school was still doing well, and as a result most of the children in the area could read and write. Following the visit, Betsy strolled back to the manor house, where she found an envelope on the table inside the main entrance. She recognized the handwriting immediately. The letter was from Joseph. Betsy frowned. Whenever Joseph was staying at Mildred's Court in London for a few days, he hardly ever corresponded with her.

Betsy picked up the envelope and turned it in her hands before opening it. "My dearest wife," Betsy read. "It is with deep regret that I inform you of the dire circumstances in London. As I write, the Bank of

England is surrounded by armed guards to prevent a forcible rush on the bank. Our bank, too, is failing, and without the intervention of Providence, there is nothing I can now do to save us."

Betsy read the letter three times. She knew there had been some financial rumblings of late because Joseph had explained them to her. As the British economy began to pick up following the end of the Napoleonic Wars, companies began looking for ways to turn profits as quickly as possible. One of the ways was by borrowing money from British banks and investing it in mining and other South American industries. The banks were willing to lend the money, sensing a very good return on their capital. Investing in South America almost became an obsession in Great Britain, so much so that a Scotsman named Gregor MacGregor made up a country in Central America that didn't even exist. MacGregor called this country "Poyais" and proceeded to sell bogus Poyais bonds in London for several hundred thousand pounds. So eager were people to invest in anything to do with South America that they didn't even bother to check whether Poyais actually existed. MacGregor even managed to convince seven shiploads of people to emigrate from England to Poyais, promising untold wealth when they arrived. MacGregor's ruse was soon uncovered when the first ship arrived to find no such country in Central America. Joseph had explained to Betsy that MacGregor's swindle, plus the fact that the promised investment returns from South America were not materializing, had made banks and investors nervous. As a result, many companies and banks were financially overextended. Joseph had thought the situation would correct itself, but it did not. Fry's Bank was once again on the brink of financial collapse.

That night Joseph returned to Plashet along with Betsy's brothers Joseph John and Samuel and her brother-in-law Fowell. The four men and Betsy met late into the night, discussing ways in which Fry's Bank might be shored up financially. The following weeks were nerve-wracking for everyone. Financial agreements were made that fell through, and then different arrangements were made. Most of the banks in England were in similar situations, and in the end, sixty of them failed. But with help from the Gurneys, Fry's Bank was secured. But for how long? Betsy did not know. Her brothers had been firm. This was the last time they would bail out Joseph Fry and his bank. If he got into financial difficulty again, there would be no rescue.

With the financial crisis averted, Joseph struggled on with the family business while Betsy concentrated on her reform work. She traveled throughout England, preaching at meetings, visiting prisons, and setting up women's committees. Betsy also continued to visit each convict ship that left England for Australia, making sure the women had what they needed for the long voyage.

In February 1827, Betsy and her brother Joseph John set out on a short sea voyage of their own—to Ireland. Their plan was to travel throughout the place, speaking and visiting prisons and insane asylums to produce a report for Parliament. When she arrived in Dublin, Betsy found that her reputation had preceded her. Thousands of Irish people flocked to hear her speak. Often several hundred of them had to be turned away because the meeting halls were filled to capacity. It was not just Protestants that came to hear her. Catholics also poured into the meeting venues. When she was not speaking, it was not uncommon for one hundred or more people to show up at the hotel each day seeking a private meeting with Betsy, who tried to accommodate as many of them as she could. When she wasn't having private audiences with people, Betsy and Joseph John visited prisons, insane asylums, and hospitals.

As she made these visits, Betsy was particularly impressed with the asylums, which were different from anything she had experienced in England. The Irish asylums, particularly those in and around Dublin, were orderly and comfortable, and the patients were treated with a respect unheard of in England. The patients were well cared for and given useful things to do during the day. The Irish prisons, though, were far worse than the prisons in England. Betsy was particularly concerned at the way debtors in Irish prisons were treated. As they traveled the length and breadth of Ireland, Betsy and Joseph John helped to set up women's associations, much like Betsy's Newgate association, with committees of women who dedicated themselves to improving the conditions inside Ireland's prisons.

In May, when Betsy returned home to Plashet from her Ireland trip, she was told her sister Rachel was seriously ill with tuberculosis, the same disease that had claimed the life of their sister Priscilla. Betsy rushed to be at Rachel's side and nurse her as best she could. It was heartbreaking to see her sister's health steadily decline. Betsy knew that Rachel was dying and that nothing could be done to turn back the disease. Despite her sister's grave condition, Betsy was amazed at how Rachel was a Christian inspiration to many. When she was near death, Rachel told her sisters, "I have had trials of body, but do not know when I have been so free from trials of mind: they are turned or are turning into gold."

Rachel Gurney died on September 16, 1827. The following day, Betsy's daughter, Rachel Cresswell, gave birth to another son. As so often before, life and death were entwined.

Following the death of her sister and the birth of her grandson, Betsy returned to Plashet, where a pile of letters awaited her attention. She noted that many of the letters had come from continental Europe. One of the letters caught her attention: it was from the empress of Russia, who explained how she had been so impressed with John Venning's report on insane asylums in Russia that she had taken it upon herself to make sure the conditions in the asylums were improved. It astonished Betsy that her influence was being felt as far away as Russia.

Throughout the following year, Betsy continued to keep busy with her prison reform work. By now her oldest daughter, Kitty, had taken over the daily running of the Fry household, freeing Betsy from the huge task. And during the year, Betsy's third daughter, Richenda, married Foster Reynolds in a large and joyful wedding.

As 1828 drew on, the disaster that had been lurking in the shadows finally overcame Betsy and Joseph. Fry's Bank was once again encountering financial difficulty, and this time no one came to the rescue. The bank stopped trading on November 21, 1828. It was over. The wealthy lifestyle Betsy and Joseph had enjoyed was gone. Bailiffs from the court arrived at Plashet, walking through the manor house and taking note of anything valuable that could be sold to pay off the family's debts. The house itself would have to be vacated and sold, and Joseph was forced to declare bankruptcy.

By January 1829 almost everything that Elizabeth and Joseph Fry owned had been sold at auction, and the family had moved to The Cedars on Upton Lane. This house, which was much smaller than Plashet, sat on Betsy's brother Sam's estate in Essex. Betsy sighed as she moved in, leaving behind her days of entertaining large groups of people.

Other changes had also taken place. Since no more income was coming from the bank, the Gurney brothers offered to pay Betsy a monthly allowance, urging her to retire from public life and live out the rest of her days quietly.

Worse was to come. Betsy and her children watched powerlessly as the Quakers shunned Joseph. While Betsy remained in good standing with the group, Joseph was disowned because of his bankruptcy. Betsy had suspected such action would be taken against her husband. Many Quakers were involved in business and banking, and the reputation of the group rested upon every Quaker's business dealings being above reproach. Nonetheless, the Quaker reaction was a harsh blow for the entire family. Three of the Frys' adult children, Rachel, John, and William, turned away from the religious group they had been raised among. This greatly disturbed Betsy at first, but she came to accept it, and then to understand it. She began to question some of the harsher Quaker practices and contrasted them with the loving support she received from her friends and relatives who were members of the Church of England.

As always, Betsy poured her thoughts into her diary.

> The longer I live, the more difficult do I see education to be; more particularly, as it respects to the religious restraints that we put upon our children. To do enough and not too much is a most delicate and important point. I begin seriously to doubt whether as it respects the particular scruples of Friends, it is not better quite to leave sober-minded young persons to judge for themselves. . . . It matters not what name we call ourselves by, or what outward means we may think right to use, if our hearts are but influenced by the love of Christ, cleansed by His baptism and strengthened by His Spirit.

Despite her disappointment at the actions of the Quakers, with financial help and encouragement from her brothers and sisters and William Wilberforce, Betsy carried on. Yet she was aware that many others judged her harshly because of the bank failure. "I still hear from different quarters evil reports of me. . . . I have been raised up in no common degree and cast down in no common degree," she wrote.

As she adjusted to her new, more humble life, Betsy had one overriding question: What would the world make of the fact that Great Britain's most famous Quaker and prison reformer was bankrupt? Would she be able to carry on with her work? Betsy decided there was only one way to find out: put the bankruptcy behind her and get back to her reform work.

Chapter 14

Multiplying Influence

While Betsy was no longer Mrs. Fry the lady of Plashet, she soon discovered that the British public still thought of and respected her as Elizabeth Fry of Newgate Prison. As a result, her reform work carried on, but not without its critics. Even radical thinkers like Sydney Smith, who championed the rights of slaves and women, felt that Betsy's compassion for prisoners went too far. He wrote to the newspaper about what he would do differently at the jail.

> We would banish all looms . . . and substitute nothing but the tread-wheel or capstan, or some species of labour where the prisoner could not see the result of his toil—where it was as monotonous, irksome and dull as possible—pulling and pushing, instead of

> reading and writing—no share of the profits—not a shilling. There should be no tea and sugar—no assemblage of female felons around the washtub—nothing but beating hemp and pulling oakum, and pounding bricks—no work but what was tedious, unusual and unfeminine. . . . Mrs. Fry is an amiable excellent woman . . . but hers is not the method to stop crimes. In prisons . . . there must be a great deal of solitude; coarse food; a dress of shame; hard, incessant, irksome, eternal labour; a planned and regulated and unrelenting exclusion of happiness and comfort.

Despite the public criticism, Betsy always had her eyes on the prize of reestablishing women convicts in society, where they could live meaningful and productive lives. She knew that the women needed new skills and lots of encouragement to accomplish this when they left prison.

Not only had Betsy's circumstances changed, but also England itself was undergoing changes. One of these changes meant that members of the Metropolitan Police Force now patrolled the streets of London. Betsy was grateful to Home Secretary Robert Peel for this. Peel had written the Metropolitan Police Act, which was passed by Parliament in 1829. The act established the new police force, whose members were soon being referred to as "peelers" after him. The new force consisted of one thousand officers, all at least six feet tall, dressed in blue tailcoats and top hats and carrying in a long pocket in their coattail a truncheon, a pair of handcuffs, and a wooden rattle to raise the alarm. The Metropolitan Police Force's job was to control crime and disorder on the streets of London. The members of the force were to be conspicuous on the streets by carrying out regular patrols. They were also charged with investigating crimes, determining who committed them, arresting and putting those people in jail, and if possible recovering any stolen property.

Another change came in June 1830 when King George IV died, leaving his sixty-four-year-old brother William to succeed him to the throne. Because William IV and his wife, Queen Adelaide, had no living children together, William's eleven-year-old niece, Princess Victoria, became the next in line for the British throne.

As soon as it could be arranged, Betsy paid a call on the young princess and her mother, the widowed Duchess of Kent. Betsy presented Princess Victoria with several books about the abolition of slavery in the British Empire, hoping that she would become a champion of that cause when she eventually became Queen of England.

New challenges were always on the horizon, with Betsy there to meet some of them. In early 1832 a cholera epidemic that had ravaged Russia, Hungary, and Germany was brought to England by sailors arriving from the European continent. People were terrified of the "blue death" that could strike and kill healthy people in a matter of hours. In response to the crisis, Betsy organized a group of women to nurse the sick. Meanwhile Parliament declared March 21, 1832, a national Day of Fasting and Humiliation for

God to stop the disease. While Betsy believed in the power of prayer, she wasn't so sure a government decreeing a day for its citizens to stop and pray would make much difference. To make a difference, people needed to pray regularly each day and believe that God would hear their prayers.

On the Day of Fasting and Humiliation, Betsy had other things on her mind. Once again she had been summoned to appear before a committee of the House of Commons on the subject of prisons. The problem was a pressing one. Since he'd become the home secretary in 1823, Robert Peel had worked relentlessly to reduce the number of offenses that led to the death penalty. During that time one hundred capital offenses had been taken off the list. This meant fewer executions and more convicts being locked away in prison. In the past, many of these prisoners would have been sent to Australia, but circumstances had changed. By now Australia had been used as a penal colony for forty-five years, and many of the convicts had served their sentences and gone on to start respectable lives. This in turn had attracted English immigrants to Australia, making new convicts less welcome on the huge continent. It was clear that transportation of convicts to Australia would soon end and Great Britain would have to house more prisoners in the nation's jails than ever before. Also, the peelers were proving to be effective in solving crimes and arresting felons, adding to an increasing jail population. As a result, many new prisons needed to be built, and with them decisions had to be made.

The need for more prisons led to difficult questions. What was the purpose of locking up a prisoner? Was it to stop prisoners from committing more crimes, punishing them for the crime committed, or for prisoners to see the error of their ways and be returned back to society better—reformed—people? In the nineteen years since she had stepped into Newgate Prison, Betsy had formed some very definite opinions on these questions. She believed that prisons should rehabilitate prisoners and that while in prison, convicts should be educated, treated fairly, not exposed to other prisoners who had committed far worse crimes, and taught skills that would help them fit back into normal society when they were discharged. She spoke passionately about these issues before the parliamentary committee, but one issue that alarmed her more than any other was a new idea that had arrived from the United States. Worst of all, it was labeled a "Quaker solution."

Betsy was aware that the British government had sent William Crawford, who was active with Sam and Fowell in the Society for the Reformation of Prison Discipline, to the United States to see how that nation was dealing with convicts and prisons. William came back with a glowing report on the methods used in the three-year-old Eastern Penitentiary at Cherry Hill, Pennsylvania. The method used there was called the "silent and separate system," in which each prisoner had his own windowless cell with only a Bible to read. The prisoner left his cell once a day to exercise alone in the yard. During their entire sentence, up to ten or more years, prisoners did not see anyone except their jailers. William Crawford explained enthusiastically that the idea behind this system was to give prisoners plenty of time to think about what they had done wrong and why they should mend their ways when released.

The notion repulsed Betsy. She had toured many jails in Great Britain where men and women were kept in solitary confinement, and some of these prisoners had gone mad as a result. "How," she asked the members of the committee, "would any person be better suited to return to lawful work after sitting alone for years at a time?"

Betsy's brother-in-law Sam Hoare had sided with William in the debate, and eventually Betsy lost the argument. The first new prison to be built in England would be based on the model used in Pennsylvania and would have tiny, separate cells where prisoners could be kept in isolation.

The defeat was depressing, one that Betsy was sure would need to be corrected in the future. Nonetheless, Betsy continued her work, again visiting Irish prisons and asylums in August 1832. Also in 1832, Betsy and Joseph's son William married Juliana Pelly, whose father was the governor of the Hudson's Bay Company. Once again, one of the Frys' children had married outside the Quakers.

Although now fifty-two years old and in poor health, Betsy drove herself on. She visited the island of Jersey to recuperate from an illness in the summer and fall of 1833. As she had nine years before while recuperating in Brighton, Betsy found ways to help the local community. The island of Jersey, one of the Channel Islands which lay between England and France, was a British Crown dependency, yet it had not been caught up in the wave of reforms sweeping across Great Britain. Betsy visited the prisons, hospitals, and asylums on Jersey and the other Channel Islands, cataloging inmates and patients and suggesting improvements that could be made, such as providing better menus and longer exercise times for prisoners and teaching prisoners useful crafts.

While recuperating on Jersey, Betsy received the news that her friend, supporter, and fellow reformer William Wilberforce had died in London on July 29, 1833, at the age of seventy-three. The news saddened Betsy, who would miss her old friend. At the time of his death, Wilberforce, along with Betsy's brother-in-law Fowell, had been working on one last great reform—a parliamentary bill that would abolish slavery throughout the British Empire. The House of Commons had already passed the bill. Betsy was delighted to learn that a month after Wilberforce's death and in his honor, the House of Lords, the upper chamber of the British Parliament, passed the Slavery Abolition Bill, abolishing slavery throughout the British Empire by August 1, 1834.

Following her time of recuperation on Jersey, Betsy headed back to England, where she busied herself with prison reform work and her ongoing commitment at Newgate Prison.

In early 1835 Betsy was again called to give evidence before a select committee, this time of the House of Lords. Again Betsy pointed out the need for more prison reform along the lines of what she had accomplished with the women prisoners at Newgate. She highlighted the importance of the Christian faith in prisoners' lives, and not just having prisoners locked in isolation with only a Bible to read. She stressed the need to have people explain the Christian faith to prisoners and help them to put it into practice in their lives.

In April 1836 Betsy made another trip to Ireland, this time to visit the first prison in the British Isles built specifically for women at Grange Gorman Lane in Dublin. The authorities in Dublin recognized Betsy's expertise in handling women prisoners. Betsy had many meetings with them to explain step-by-step how the approaches she had pioneered at Newgate Prison should be implemented in the new jail.

In September 1836 Betsy was invited back to the island of Jersey, where a new house of correction was being built. Betsy was overjoyed to be back on Jersey. She felt the prison reforms were a result of the work she had done highlighting conditions in the Channel Islands while she recuperated on Jersey three years before.

Bad news followed. Betsy's sister Louisa Hoare was seriously ill. Betsy rushed back to England while Joseph, Kitty, and their servant, Mary, continued on to France. Betsy planned to join them there once she had attended to Louisa. In France she hoped to meet with some of the people with whom she had been corresponding over the years. By the time Betsy reached her sister's side, there was little hope. Louisa was paralyzed from a stroke and unable to speak. She died soon after Betsy's arrival, and with her passing another link to Betsy's old life was lost.

Although distraught by Louisa's death, Betsy headed for France for an informal first visit to the country. She arrived in Calais, where her husband met her. Joseph looked terrible, and he told Betsy how the carriage he, Kitty, and Mary had been traveling in had broken a wheel, rolled over, and tumbled down a ravine. Although none of them were seriously injured, they were all bruised and shaken. Betsy was beginning to wonder whether the family's troubles would ever end.

In northern France, Betsy attended prison reform discussions and visited as many prisons as she was able. At Saint-Omer she visited a school and hospital run by Roman Catholic nuns. She hadn't known what to expect of this visit, and she was deeply touched by the dedication and sacrifice of the nuns, so much so that she wrote, "The sacrifice that must be made to give up the whole life, as the Sisters of Charity do to teach and bring up the poor children and attend to the sick in their hospitals, is very exemplary." She wondered if the nuns' approach might be a beneficial approach for Protestants.

Back in England in 1837, Betsy faced the loss of still another relative. This time it was Lady Harriet Gurney, her brother Daniel's wife, who died, leaving her husband with eight young children to care for. Betsy consoled the family as best she could and then proceeded to King's Lynn, where her daughter Rachel and her husband now lived. Rachel was about to give birth to another baby, and Betsy came to help her. While at King's Lynn, a Quaker couple arranged for Betsy to preach at a local Methodist chapel. The meeting was a huge success, but the aftermath was not. Rachel was hysterical that her mother had left her side to go and preach, and she accused Betsy of making a public spectacle of herself among their Anglican friends, who did not approve of women preaching. Betsy felt terrible that her actions had upset her daughter so much. After attending Rachel through the birth of her baby, she wearily returned home to Upton Lane in Essex.

Back at home it was Joseph's turn to complain. In his opinion, his wife was neglecting him, spending more time on her causes than she did on her marriage. Betsy was crestfallen and promised to do better, but she wondered what she could change. As summer 1837 drew near, she now had twenty grandchildren to care for, with many more sure to be born, and there was the prison reform work to keep on track, as well as the correspondence from people all over the United Kingdom and Europe who begged Betsy to give them advice or, better yet, to come and visit.

Over the summer Betsy traveled to Liverpool to see her brother Joseph John off as he set sail for the United States. Joseph John had desperately wanted her to go with him on the trip, and Betsy was tempted, but she was afraid her family would fall apart if she were to leave them.

On the trip home, Betsy experienced a new marvel. She took a steam train from Liverpool to Birmingham. It was the first time Betsy had traveled faster than a horse could run. She did not enjoy the experience at all, noting in her diary that objects were speeding by the window too fast for her to take a proper look at them. She also noted that the "noise is deafening, the motion jarring, particles of cinders or iron dust get into your eyes and blind you for the time and make your eyes weak for a day or two afterward." Yet as she traveled on the train, Betsy was astonished at how the British landscape was changing. Giant factories with tall brick chimneys belching black smoke were springing up all around. The truth was, the steam engine that pulled the train along was just one part of a great industrial revolution transforming England.

On June 20, 1837, King William IV died at the age of seventy-one, and with his death Princess Victoria became Queen of the United Kingdom, ushering in the beginning of the Victorian Era. Betsy remembered meeting the new queen as a young princess, and she had high hopes that the eighteen-year-old monarch would reform many parts of English life.

In January 1838, Betsy and Joseph Fry set out on their first *official* visit to France. In Paris they stayed at the Hotel de Castille, and as news quickly spread that Elizabeth Fry was in Paris, a steady stream of visitors began arriving at the hotel. The visitors consisted of a wide assortment of people. Some came from aristocratic French families, others were government officials, and still others came from more humble backgrounds. Regardless of who came to meet her, after formalities Betsy always turned the conversation to prison reform.

Betsy was also the guest of honor at a formal dinner given by Lord and Lady Granville at the British Embassy in Paris. As the well-heeled guests at the dinner listened to Betsy speak about her work and the importance of the Christian faith in turning around the lives of prisoners, many were moved to tears. What seemed so natural and normal to Betsy seemed extraordinary to the guests.

While in Paris, Betsy visited a number of prisons. One of them was Saint-Lazare, which housed 952 female prisoners. Walking into this institution, Betsy felt as she had when she walked into Newgate Prison for the first time. The conditions were primitive and the smell overpowering. As she had done at Newgate and many other British prisons, Betsy stood before the women prisoners and spoke to them. First the parable of the prodigal son was read from a French Bible, and then Betsy drew parallels between the parable and the prisoner's lives. The prison warden translated her words into French. Betsy went on to tell the prisoners about her work at Newgate and the change that had taken place there. Finally she asked if the women would like something similar to happen among them in Saint-Lazare. "*Oui*," one prisoner said, and then a chorus of "*Moi aussi* [me too]" came from the other women prisoners. Betsy spoke to the governor of the prison and a number of the Parisian women who had accompanied her on the visit, and plans were made to establish a program in Saint-Lazare similar to that at Newgate.

Betsy's final official engagement in Paris, which occurred on March 2, 1838, was a meeting with the king and queen of France and the Duchess of Orleans. At the meeting Betsy discussed the need for not just prison reform but also educational reform in France. She presented the king and queen with a copy of the book on education her sister Louisa had written, along with several books on prison reform written by her brother Joseph John. The king's sister, Princess Adelaide, promised she would read the books.

Betsy returned to England, and a year later in March, she returned to France with Joseph and their eldest daughter, Kitty, and youngest son, Daniel. For this visit Betsy had been issued an official permit to visit all the prisons in France so that she could write a full report on what was going on in French jails. For six months the group traveled the length and breadth of France, documenting prison conditions and suggesting improvements and reforms in the way prisoners were housed and treated.

In February 1840 Betsy made another visit to Europe, this time accompanied by her brother Samuel and his daughter, Elizabeth, along with two Quaker Friends. Before leaving, Betsy and Samuel had an audience with Queen Victoria. Betsy wanted to have a long conversation with the queen about prison reform but instead was allowed only to answer the questions the queen asked her. Betsy was frustrated to be so close to such a powerful figure and yet be unable to speak her mind. Many others, however, from all walks of life were eager to hear Betsy speak. Betsy preached to a crowd of over fifteen hundred people before embarking on the first leg of her trip across the English Channel to Ostend, Belgium. Betsy and her four companions intended to spend four months on the European continent, traveling by coach to Brussels, Antwerp, Amsterdam, and Berlin, covering a distance of nearly one thousand miles.

The people of Belgium, along with the king, enthusiastically welcomed Betsy, who was given free rein to inspect the nation's prisons, schools, and hospitals. Betsy also spoke at public meetings and gave private audiences. She met with Belgium's king, who was greatly touched by her work with prisoners.

From Belgium they traveled on to Holland, where a similar welcome awaited Betsy. Then it was on to Berlin, where Betsy was given a royal reception. Princess William (called after her husband, as customary) agreed to be the patron of the Berlin Association for the Improvement of Female Offenders, which Betsy helped to found. As sister-in-law of the king of Prussia and longtime first lady, Princess William was an excellent ally. Following her stay, Betsy traveled to the small town of Kaiserswerth, six miles north of Düsseldorf on the Rhine River. She met with Theodor Fliedner, a Lutheran clergyman, whom she had met six years before in London when he came to observe her work at Newgate Prison. Theodor had been impressed by what he saw, and he and Betsy had begun corresponding.

Betsy was amazed by what she found in Kaiserswerth. Theodor had founded the Rhenish-Westphalian Prison Association. He explained that he had visited prisons throughout the region and put pressure on officials to reform them. He and his wife had also set up a refuge in their garden to house discharged women prisoners. He had also opened a school for children in the impoverished town. Not content with his prison work and the school, Theodor had also established a hospital where deaconesses, a new Protestant equivalent to Catholic nuns, were being trained as nurses while they ministered to female patients. Betsy was in awe of how efficiently the hospital was run and the quality of young women Theodor had attracted to become nurses. All that Betsy saw in Kaiserswerth humbled her. She wondered how many more endeavors like this there might be in other countries started by people who had visited her in England or with whom she corresponded regularly. It suddenly made the drudgery of writing hundreds of letters to people she did not know seem worthwhile.

On May 21, 1840, a few days after visiting Theodor in Kaiserswerth, Betsy turned sixty. It was a time of reflection. Betsy had accomplished so many things, and she knew she had only a little more left to give. The question became, where should she spend her remaining energy?

As she jostled along in the carriage heading back toward Ostend and eventually England, Betsy found her mind wandering back to Kaiserswerth and the wonderfully trained nurses caring for sick patients. She wondered what it would take to find dedicated, intelligent, and kind women in England who would be willing to train as nurses. It was an interesting question, one Betsy was determined to find an answer to.

Chapter 15

"Death Itself There Dies"

When she arrived back in England, Betsy was still impressed by all she had experienced in Kaiserswerth, particularly the training of nurses there. As soon as she had settled back at The Cedars on Upton Lane, Betsy set to work. Within several weeks she had founded Protestant Nurses, the first-of-its-kind training program in Great Britain. Up until this time, nurses, who did much of the menial work in British hospitals, were drawn from the ranks of destitute women who could find no other work. Often these nurses would be intoxicated and dirty, walking out on patients and not following a doctor's instructions. Betsy wanted to change this. She wanted to produce nurses who were well trained, motivated, caring, clean, and sober.

To help her with the task, Betsy enlisted the aid of her brother Samuel's wife, Elizabeth. She also won the support of both the queen's mother and Lady Inglis, another prominent woman, as patrons. Once the organizational details were taken care of, Betsy began interviewing women—who had to be single or widowed—wanting to become nurses. She selected twenty of these women, who could all read and write and owned a Bible. Once the nurse candidates were chosen, Betsy handed over the details of their training to others. Her sister-in-law Elizabeth made arrangements for the women to be trained as nurses at various hospitals throughout London.

As the Protestant Nurses training program got under way, Betsy had many other things to busy herself with. In June 1840 she headed to Exeter Hall in London to attend the first World Anti-Slavery Convention, where she was to speak. Betsy's interest had been drawn to the antislavery cause years before through her close ties with William Wilberforce and her brother-in-law Thomas Fowell Buxton. Betsy was twenty-seven years old when slave trading was outlawed in the British Empire, and she was fifty-four when, a month after Wilberforce's death, the Slavery Abolition Bill was passed in 1833, freeing about 800,000 slaves throughout the British Empire when the act came into force the next year. Now a new antislavery society, made up mainly of Quakers, was meeting to put pressure on other countries in the world to abolish slavery.

Three thousand convention attendees rose to their feet and clapped loudly as Betsy made her way onto the stage. Looking out over the audience, Betsy saw how few women were in attendance. Betsy knew this was a sore spot. Some of the delegates, like Elizabeth Cady Stanton and Lucretia Mott, a fellow Quaker preacher, had traveled all the way from the United States to take part in the proceedings, and some of the men running the convention had refused to let them speak. This left Betsy in a bind. As the most well-known woman in England after the queen, Betsy had such an impressive reputation that the men dared not ban her from the stage. But other, less well-known women attendees were not made to feel welcome at the convention.

During the proceedings Betsy met with Elizabeth Cady Stanton and Lucretia Mott to apologize for the inadequate welcome they received. Although Lucretia Mott was understanding about the situation, Elizabeth Cady Stanton was not. She confided to Betsy that her reception at the convention had convinced her she needed to fight not only for the freedom of slaves but also for the rights of women.

In August, soon after the World Anti-Slavery Convention, Betsy traveled to Portsmouth in the south of England to greet her brother Joseph John upon his returning from three years of traveling in the United States and the Caribbean. While waiting for the ship to arrive, she could not resist visiting a new prison for boys on the nearby Isle of Wight.

When the ship from the United States docked, Betsy was delighted to find Joseph John in good spirits. The two of them had much to tell each other as they made their way from Portsmouth to the Earlham estate. Betsy told her brother about how Fowell had just been knighted for his effort toward ending the slave trade, about the Protestant Nurses (or Fry Nurses, as they were now commonly called) and about the Patronage Society she had helped to start to find honest work for newly released prisoners.

For his part, Joseph John talked about how important it was to end slavery in the southern United States and in the Caribbean Islands, where he had spent a winter. He told Betsy that he wanted to go to the European continent the following year and confront the kings and queens of a number of countries over the issue of slavery in their colonies. He asked Betsy to accompany him and help him with introductions to the royal houses. Betsy was reluctant at first—she had not been feeling well since her return to England from the Continent several months before. However, the thought of joining forces with her brother soon captured her imagination.

On July 31, 1841, Betsy, Joseph John, his daughter Anna, and Samuel's daughter Elizabeth set out on a tour of Europe. Although on previous visits Betsy had crisscrossed the Continent by coach, this time she traveled by rail. The European countryside whizzed by as they rode the train to The Hague in the Netherlands to visit the recently crowned king, William II, and his wife, queen consort Anna Pavlovna. Anna was the youngest sister of the czar of Russia, and she confided to Betsy that her influence had been felt all the way to Russia. Joseph John spoke to the royal couple about how freed slaves in the British West Indies in the Caribbean had helped the islands to prosper. He urged King William II to consider freeing the slaves under his control in Surinam and the Dutch West

Indies. Later that night Joseph John spoke to a group of prominent Dutch businessmen about the advantages of letting the slaves go free and paying them a working wage instead.

From Holland the group took the train to the German city of Bremen, where they caught a ferryboat across the Baltic Sea to Copenhagen to meet with the king and queen of Denmark. Betsy used the opportunity to talk to the royal couple about her usual subjects of prison reform and the freeing of slaves. She also addressed another issue that had caught her attention: the persecution of religious groups. In England, many restrictions against Christian groups dissenting from the official Church of England had been lifted, some during Betsy's own lifetime. The English dissenters, or nonconformists, included Puritans, Baptists, Presbyterians, Methodists, and Quakers, among many others. Now, as Betsy traveled, she saw continued religious persecution firsthand.

In Denmark Betsy toured a prison, where she talked with two brothers, Peter and Adolph Muster, who told her they were both Baptist ministers. Denmark's state church was Lutheran, and the brothers were being held in solitary confinement for their Baptist beliefs. Betsy knew she had to do something to help them. She returned to visit the king of Denmark and strongly urged him to free the two brothers. The king honored her request and let the men go.

The tour continued on through Hamburg, Hannover, Berlin, Dresden, and Halle. At each stop Betsy and Joseph John visited prisons, schools, and asylums and met with royalty and high government officials. Along the way Betsy began to suspect that she was becoming seriously ill. She took longer to get out of bed in the mornings and fought the urge to sleep throughout the day. By the time they reached Silesia, she was finding it difficult to move around.

Joseph John confided that he was worried about her and knew he needed to get England's most famous reformer back home in one piece as quickly as possible. Besides, he needed to get home himself, as he was to be married in three weeks. He hired a stagecoach and six strong horses to take them back to the coast to catch a boat for England. Betsy spent most of the trip to the coast lying on a padded board in the stagecoach. Every bump and turn in the road was painful for her. After ten weeks of traveling on the European continent, Betsy was glad when they arrived back in Dover, England.

Following their return from Europe, Joseph John Gurney, twice widowed, married Eliza Kirkbride, an American Quaker whom he had traveled with in the United States. Betsy was delighted with the match, and the entire Fry and Gurney families welcomed Eliza with open arms.

Betsy remained unwell, and her children took turns nursing her in their homes. Her oldest daughter, Kitty, stayed with Betsy most of the time, helping her to answer the bags of mail that continued to arrive. During this time Betsy mustered the strength to meet with a number of distinguished visitors. Chevalier Bunsen, the Prussian ambassador, visited her, as did Lady Pirie, one of the staunchest supporters of Betsy's work at Newgate Prison. Lady Pirie's husband, John Pirie, was a leading shipbroker in

London who had recently been made the Lord Mayor of London. Lady Pirie also invited Betsy to attend a banquet to mark the start of the building of the new Royal Exchange, the old exchange having burned down four years before.

Betsy felt well enough to attend the occasion, at which Prince Albert, Queen Victoria's husband, laid the foundation stone for the new exchange. At the banquet Betsy was seated between Prince Albert and Sir Robert Peel. She had a wonderful time with the prince, expressing her views on childrearing and Christian family values, and with Robert Peel, discussing further prison reform ideas.

The banquet was followed by more royal encounters. Less than two weeks later, on January 25, 1842, Queen Victoria's first son, Albert Edward, was christened, and King Frederick IV of Prussia, who had given Betsy a royal reception in Berlin two years before, arrived in London to become the godfather of the young Prince of Wales. While in London, King Frederick invited Betsy and Joseph to a banquet held in his honor at the Mansion House. In return, the king asked to visit Newgate Prison with Betsy and also to dine with the Fry family at their home on Upton Lane. Betsy gladly agreed to both requests, although she knew that many of her Plain Quaker friends would question her motives in entertaining royalty.

On the morning of January 31, Betsy met King Frederick at the Mansion House. Her brother Sam and his wife, Elizabeth, along with Lady Pirie, some sheriffs, and other dignitaries, also assembled there, and Betsy led them all in a procession to Newgate

Prison. Betsy had arranged for refreshments to be served to the guests while she explained to the king how the prisoners at Newgate were treated when she first visited the prison twenty-nine years before. The king wanted to see everything, and he took Betsy by the arm as she led him deep into the bowels of the prison, pointing out improvements that had been made over the years. In one area sixty women inmates and a large group from the Association for the Improvement of the Female Prisoners in Newgate waited eagerly for them. Betsy introduced the king and addressed the crowd. "Remember that the King of kings and Lord of lords is present, in whose fear we should abide." Then she knelt down on the stones and prayed for them all.

The king patted Betsy's arm on the way back to the prison gates. "*You* are my favorite saint," he told her.

The next day everything at The Cedars on Upton Lane was ready for the arrival of the king. Once again, Betsy knew that many of her religious friends thought she was being vain for entertaining such an important man in her home, but Betsy saw things differently. She felt that her social position was a gift from God and that she should use it to try to influence as many leaders as possible to treat those under their rule with dignity and respect.

The visit by King Frederick was one that neither Betsy nor anyone in her family would ever forget. All Betsy's children, except Rachel, who was in France with her sick husband, greeted the king in the Frys' drawing room. Twenty-five grandchildren assembled in one of the bedrooms, waiting to be introduced to the king once he finished dining. The king warmly greeted everyone in the family, and during lunch he regaled them with stories from Europe. Then he was introduced to each of Betsy's grandchildren. When it was time to leave, he wept. "This is exactly as I imagined it to be," he told Betsy, "my favorite saint surrounded by a loving and devoted family."

The king's visit proved to be the highlight of a long and difficult year for Betsy, whose health continued to decline. In December Betsy's eight-year-old granddaughter, Harriet Streatfeild, died. And then right before Christmas, her brother Joseph John was diagnosed with diabetes.

Eager to make the next year count, Joseph John encouraged Betsy to tour Europe with him and his wife, Eliza. Betsy agreed to go. The traveling group included Betsy's daughter Kitty as well as Josiah Forster, an elder among the British Quakers and an early member of the British and Foreign Anti-Slavery Society. It was Josiah's brother William who thirty years earlier, along with Stephen Grellet, had introduced Betsy to her prison ministry. When the group left for Europe in April 1843, Betsy hoped the change of air would invigorate her. It did not. The passage across the English Channel was rough, and almost immediately Betsy began to wonder whether she had done the right thing. When she reached Paris, the city held none of its old charm. The days were long and hot, and Betsy struggled to get out of bed in the mornings. Still, she did what she could, visiting old friends and making new ones. She talked with a large group of black medical students who were former slaves in Haiti and Guadeloupe, and she spoke to twenty-two Catholic nuns about her faith and her efforts to reform Newgate Prison.

On May 21, 1843, Betsy celebrated her sixty-third birthday. The queen of France sent her a beautiful Bible to commemorate the day. The following month Betsy was grateful to be home once more in England.

By the spring of 1844 Betsy was feeling quite unwell, and she suspected that she would not recover from this bout of illness. All around her, other friends and family members were ill or dying as well. She visited Bath with Fowell and Hannah Buxton. Fowell was ill and wanted to bathe in the mineral waters there. While there, Betsy learned that her sister-in-law, Joseph's sister Elizabeth, had died.

By now Betsy realized that her days of preaching and ministering at Quaker meetings was over, yet she yearned to attend one more Quaker meeting at the Plaistow Quaker meetinghouse, which she had attended when living at Plashet. Her son William carried her from the carriage and placed her gently into a wheelchair so that she could be pushed through the old, familiar doors of the meetinghouse. Betsy's wheelchair was positioned next to the bench where for many years she had sat beside her now-deceased sister-in-law, Elizabeth. Memories flooded back as Betsy sat in silence during the meeting. After some time she felt moved to speak. Betsy quoted the text, "Blessed are the dead which die in the Lord from henceforth, . . . that they may cease from their labours; and their works do follow them" (Revelation 14:13).

More deaths were to come. In the spring of 1844 Betsy's young grandson, Gurney Reynolds, died. Less than a month later, her son William's daughter Juliana became ill and within hours died from scarlet fever, a deadly and highly contagious disease. Then William himself contracted the disease, and he died the next week, followed by his oldest daughter, Emma. It was a strong blow to Betsy to lose three grandchildren and her son in such a short period of time. She wept for those left behind and took comfort in a poem by Samuel Taylor Coleridge that her brother Joseph John sent her. The last lines of the poem read,

> Is that a death-bed, where a Christian lies?
> Yes! But not his—'tis Death itself there dies.

The following spring, Betsy's beloved brother-in-law Sir Thomas Fowell Buxton died at the age of fifty-nine. Fowell had stood at Betsy's side so many times in the fight for prison reform and against slavery. Betsy knew she would miss him deeply. Sadly, she was not well enough to attend his burial. Instead she wrote to her sister Hannah, Fowell's widow, "I live with you in heart by night and day my tenderly beloved sister. . . . I am with you in spirit."

In early June, Betsy and Joseph went to Runcton in the south of England to visit their newly widowed daughter-in-law, William's wife, Juliana. While in Runcton, Betsy learned that her youngest son, Daniel, was going to marry Lucy Sheppard. Lucy was a Quaker, and Betsy was delighted with her son's choice to be his bride. Their marriage took place on June 26, and Betsy felt well enough to invite a large number of family and friends back to the Frys' Upton Lane house to celebrate.

Following the wedding festivities, Betsy's thoughts turned to the Earlham estate, where she had spent so many happy years. She longed to see the place one more time. In August 1845, Joseph Fry and their daughter Louisa accompanied Betsy to Earlham. It was a delight for Betsy to spend time with her brother Joseph John and his wife, Eliza, and her sister Katherine, all of whom lived at Earlham Hall. Hundreds of local folk came to visit Betsy, who was taken in her wheelchair to the Quaker meetinghouse in Norwich. Memories swirled around Betsy as she thought of her and her sisters giggling through the meetings and how she loved to wear her red boots with the purple laces because it upset the Plain Quakers. She also thought of her mother's burial, and how lost she had felt after her mother's death. It all seemed so far away to her now. Who could have predicted that all her brothers and sisters would find a genuine faith in God?

From Earlham, Joseph took Betsy south to Ramsgate so she could enjoy the sea air. Betsy liked to visit the pier there and give Christian tracts to sailors. She also visited the local Coast Guard station. The Coast Guard had absorbed the old blockade stations, and Betsy was pleased to discover that one of the libraries she had set up at blockade stations twenty-one years before was still in use.

This library was one small example of what Betsy had confided to her daughter Rachel as she patiently accepted her declining health and the deaths of so many loved ones. "I can say one thing: since my heart was touched at seventeen years old, I believe I never have awakened from sleep, in sickness or in health, without my first waking thought being how I might best serve my Lord."

Now, in Ramsgate, Betsy was often surrounded by her children and grandchildren. Betsy's daughter-in-law Juliana came to stay, and Betsy formed a special bond with Juliana's son, Willie Fry. Willie had just endured the death of his father and two older sisters, and Betsy did what she could to comfort him. They read the Bible together every morning, and Willie ran along the beach in front of Betsy's window, gathering seashells for her to examine.

One morning, coming to his grandmother for their psalm reading, Willie found her much worsened. By evening it was clear that Betsy was very ill, having suffered a stroke and seizures. The next morning Betsy spoke one last time, saying slowly, "O my dear Lord, help and keep Thy servant." Before the sun rose again, on October 13, 1845, at the age of sixty-five, the Angel of Newgate drew her last breath and died.

The seamen of the Ramsgate Coast Guard Station flew their flag at half-mast as the coffin of Elizabeth Fry, the Angel of Newgate, was placed on a carriage for her final journey. Until then, the Coast Guard flag had been flown at half-mast only to mark the death of a king of England.

Huge crowds lined the roadside as Betsy's funeral procession wound along the lane at Plashet, where she had once been the mistress of the manor house, while over a thousand more stood waiting silently at the Friends' burying ground at Barking. Betsy's body was laid next to that of her little daughter and namesake Elizabeth Fry. Her brother Joseph John offered a prayer, and then the remainder of her family retired to The Cedars on Upton Lane to mourn in private. They were stunned at the hole Elizabeth Fry had left in their lives. Betsy's niece, Priscilla Buxton, recorded her feelings that day.

> We cannot expect the next generation to believe what we know of the treasure she was. . . . They may form some idea of her outward acts and capacities; they cannot know who she was personally. After seeing her in some difficult works, my feeling was, marvelous as were her gifts, the real wonder was in her Grace, her extraordinary power of loving and caring for others; the flow of the oil which in almost all others is by drops, in her was a rich ready stream, able to take in the meanest, the most unattractive, the most unrepaying; her power of condescending to the little interests of others, combined with her greatness, her high natural powers of mind, her magnitude of action. We who tasted it can never forget it, and I feel it vain to hope that our children will ever fully take it in.

Bibliography

Bardens, Dennis. *Elizabeth Fry: Britain's Second Lady on the Five-Pound Note.* London: Chanadon, 2004.

Briggs, John, Christopher Harrison, Angus McInnes, and David Vincent. *Crime and Punishment in England: An Introductory History.* New York: St. Martin's Press, 1996.

Hare, Augustus J. C. *The Gurneys of Earlham: Volumes 1 and 2.* London: George Allen, 1895.

Hatton, Jean. *Betsy: The Dramatic Biography of Prison Reformer Elizabeth Fry.* Oxford: Monarch, 2005.

Isba, Anne. *The Excellent Mrs. Fry: Unlikely Heroine.* New York: Continuum, 2010.

Northcott, Cecil. *Angel of the Prisons: The Story of Elizabeth Fry.* Cambridge, UK: Lutterworth, 1959.

Richards, Laura E. *Elizabeth Fry: The Angel of the Prisons.* New York: D. Appleton, 1916.

Savery, William. *A Journal of the Life, Travels, and Religious Labors of William Savery, a Minister of the Gospel of Christ, of the Society of Friends, Late of Philadelphia.* London: Forgotten Books, 2012.

Whitney, Janet. *Elizabeth Fry: Quaker Heroine.* Boston: Little, Brown, 1936.

About the Authors

Janet and Geoff Benge are a husband and wife writing team with more than thirty years of writing experience. Janet is a former elementary school teacher. Geoff holds a degree in history. Together they have a passion to make history come alive for a new generation of readers.

Originally from New Zealand, the Benges make their home in the Orlando, Florida, area.

Also from Janet and Geoff Benge...

More adventure-filled biographies for ages 10 to 100!

Christian Heroes: Then and Now

Gladys Aylward: The Adventure of a Lifetime • 978-1-57658-019-6
Nate Saint: On a Wing and a Prayer • 978-1-57658-017-2
Hudson Taylor: Deep in the Heart of China • 978-1-57658-016-5
Amy Carmichael: Rescuer of Precious Gems • 978-1-57658-018-9
Eric Liddell: Something Greater Than Gold • 978-1-57658-137-7
Corrie ten Boom: Keeper of the Angels' Den • 978-1-57658-136-0
William Carey: Obliged to Go • 978-1-57658-147-6
George Müller: Guardian of Bristol's Orphans • 978-1-57658-145-2
Jim Elliot: One Great Purpose • 978-1-57658-146-9
Mary Slessor: Forward into Calabar • 978-1-57658-148-3
David Livingstone: Africa's Trailblazer • 978-1-57658-153-7
Betty Greene: Wings to Serve • 978-1-57658-152-0
Adoniram Judson: Bound for Burma • 978-1-57658-161-2
Cameron Townsend: Good News in Every Language • 978-1-57658-164-3
Jonathan Goforth: An Open Door in China • 978-1-57658-174-2
Lottie Moon: Giving Her All for China • 978-1-57658-188-9
John Williams: Messenger of Peace • 978-1-57658-256-5
William Booth: Soup, Soap, and Salvation • 978-1-57658-258-9
Rowland Bingham: Into Africa's Interior • 978-1-57658-282-4
Ida Scudder: Healing Bodies, Touching Hearts • 978-1-57658-285-5
Wilfred Grenfell: Fisher of Men • 978-1-57658-292-3
Lillian Trasher: The Greatest Wonder in Egypt • 978-1-57658-305-0
Loren Cunningham: Into All the World • 978-1-57658-199-5
Florence Young: Mission Accomplished • 978-1-57658-313-5
Sundar Singh: Footprints Over the Mountains • 978-1-57658-318-0
C.T. Studd: No Retreat • 978-1-57658-288-6
Rachel Saint: A Star in the Jungle • 978-1-57658-337-1
Brother Andrew: God's Secret Agent • 978-1-57658-355-5
Clarence Jones: Mr. Radio • 978-1-57658-343-2
Count Zinzendorf: Firstfruit • 978-1-57658-262-6
John Wesley: The World His Parish • 978-1-57658-382-1
C. S. Lewis: Master Storyteller • 978-1-57658-385-2
David Bussau: Facing the World Head-on • 978-1-57658-415-6
Jacob DeShazer: Forgive Your Enemies • 978-1-57658-475-0
Isobel Kuhn: On the Roof of the World • 978-1-57658-497-2
Elisabeth Elliot: Joyful Surrender • 978-1-57658-513-9
D. L. Moody: Bringing Souls to Christ • 978-1-57658-552-8
Paul Brand: Helping Hands • 978-1-57658-536-8
Dietrich Bonhoeffer: In the Midst of Wickedness • 978-1-57658-713-3
Francis Asbury: Circuit Rider • 978-1-57658-737-9